MW01280337

Westchester County

NY

HEADQUARTERS TO THE WORLD

Westchester

County
NY
HEADQUARTERS TO THE WORLD

ROBERT A. SLAYTON

CHERBO PUBLISHING GROUP, INC.
ENCINO, CALIFORNIA

Dedication

TO SHIRLEY ZUCKER AND
IN MEMORY OF HOWARD ZUCKER
FOR ALL THE YEARS OF LOVE

The author wishes to acknowledge, for all their help:
Albert Annunziata
Alex Philippidis
Michael Lipkin

CHERBO PUBLISHING GROUP, INC.
ENCINO, CALIFORNIA

PRESIDENT Jack C. Cherbo
EXECUTIVE VICE PRESIDENT Elaine Hoffman
EDITORIAL DIRECTOR Christina M. Beausang
MANAGING FEATURE EDITOR Margaret L. Martin
SENIOR FEATURE EDITOR Tina G. Rubin
SENIOR PROFILES EDITOR J. Kelley Younger
ASSOCIATE EDITOR Sylvia Emrich-Toma
PROFILES WRITERS Camilla Denton, Beth Mattson Teig,
Nancy Smith Seigle, Paul Sonnenburg, Stan Ziemba

ART DIRECTOR/DESIGNER Peri A. Holguin
PHOTO EDITOR Theresa Brown
SALES ADMINISTRATOR Joan K. Baker
PRODUCTION SERVICES MANAGER Ellen T. Kettenbeil
ADMINISTRATIVE COORDINATOR Jahnna Biddle
EASTERN REGIONAL MANAGER Marcia Weiss
EASTERN DEVELOPMENT DIRECTOR Glen Edwards

Cherbo Publishing Group, Inc., Encino, Calif. 91316
© 2002 by Cherbo Publishing Group, Inc.
All rights reserved. Published 2002
Printed in the United States of America
Visit CPG's Web site at WWW.CHERBOPUB.COM

Library of Congress Cataloging-in-Publication Data
Slayton, Robert A.
    Westchester County, N.Y.: Headquarters to the World
Library of Congress Control Number: 2002100691
ISBN 1-882933-42-7

The information in this publication is the most recent available and has been carefully researched to ensure accuracy. Cherbo Publishing Group, Inc., cannot and does not guarantee the correctness of all the information provided and is not responsible for errors and omissions.

The County Chamber of Commerce, Inc., Westchester's largest business and professional organization, works to showcase the outstanding quality of life the county offers those who live here, work here, and make business investments here. Westchester's scenic beauty, its broad range of residential, educational, and employment choices, and its many cultural, historic, and recreational opportunities make people who reside here proud to be county residents and those outside the area interested in the county's many opportunities.

Those of us who live here often take for granted the lifestyle and economic vitality our county possesses. These have truly made Westchester among the premier counties in the United States as well. Sometimes overlooked, too, is the fact that many of the country's major national and international corporations make Westchester their home. Their presence and corporate citizenship initiatives have enriched the social and cultural fabric of Westchester's communities while contributing significantly to its economic strength.

We at the County Chamber know that Westchester shines in many ways, and as an organization that represents business, the County Chamber is well aware that our business and professional community is first-rate and second to none. From the largest of the giants to the smallest of the entrepreneurs, we are proud of our business community and the contribution it makes to Westchester.

The County Chamber of Commerce in Westchester is pleased to present this book to showcase Westchester and its many outstanding qualities. We hope it will offer those who live here a reminder of the outstanding county Westchester is and those who live elsewhere a portrait of a community worth visiting and considering as a place to live, work, or grow a business.

Marsha Gordon

Marsha Gordon
President and CEO
The County Chamber of Commerce, Inc.

Contents

Photo: Gardener's cottage at Sunnyside, © Scott Barrow Inc./stock Barrow

Corporations & Organizations

THE FOLLOWING COMPANIES HAVE MADE A VALUABLE COMMITMENT TO THE QUALITY OF THIS PUBLICATION. THE COUNTY CHAMBER OF COMMERCE GRATEFULLY ACKNOWLEDGES THEIR PARTICIPATION IN *WESTCHESTER COUNTY, N.Y.: HEADQUARTERS TO THE WORLD.*

Photo: Sugar Pond in winter, Hastings-on-Hudson, © Heath Robbins

Profiled

Part One
Westchester

County UNLIMITED POSSIBILITIES

Photo: © CORBIS Stock Market/LWA—Stephen Welstead

Chapter 1

Quality of Life

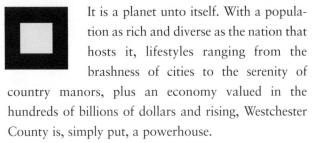

It is a planet unto itself. With a population as rich and diverse as the nation that hosts it, lifestyles ranging from the brashness of cities to the serenity of country manors, plus an economy valued in the hundreds of billions of dollars and rising, Westchester County is, simply put, a powerhouse.

In the past few years, over 1,000 companies, ranging from small start-ups to existing giants like MasterCard International, Starwood Hotels and Resorts Worldwide, and Heineken USA, moved to Westchester. The county ranks fourth among all New York counties in sales volume and number of stores. And not surprisingly, it is also fourth in terms of median income; the 1997 figure was $55,040 (the comparable figure for New York state was $36,369).

Homage to this strength came booming out of the dry pages of the U.S. Census. According to the official tally, the county's population in 2000 was 923,459, up 5.6 percent from 10 years prior. By way of comparison, New York County ("Manhattan") only grew by 3.7 percent, while neighboring Orange County came in at 3.3 percent. This was the first growth Westchester had since the 1970 count, a portent of big changes to come.

Almost all local residents are high school graduates (81 percent, compared to the state's 74.8 percent), and more than a third have a college or university diploma (35.3 percent, compared to the state's 23.1 percent). The home ownership rate is almost 60 percent, and most of the homes are single-family residences.

Westchester County also reflects the vast demographic changes shaping America today. Hispanics make up 15.6 percent of the population; blacks, 14.2 percent. There are 41,367 Asians and Pacific Islanders (3.7 percent) and 2,343 individuals with Native American ancestry.

But Westchester's diversity extends much further than numbers portray; it means lifestyle choices as well. For those seeking an urban environment, Yonkers, the biggest city in the county, has 196,066 residents, or more than half the population of St. Louis. It is, in fact, one of only five U.S. cities that turned a population loss in the eighties into a boost in the nineties, sharing this honor with such titans as Chicago, Memphis, Denver, and Atlanta.

While Yonkers provides the zip and panache of a growing metropolis, Lewisboro has a population density of only 494 persons per square mile, an almost rural lifestyle. In Pound Ridge, the density goes down to 196 per square mile. Not surprisingly, Westchester is still one of the most heavily forested places in the state, abounding in parks, campgrounds, and hiking trails.

The county seat, White Plains, is a particularly interesting place. By night it is just a small suburban city with 50,000 residents; during the day, people flock to its offices, corporate headquarters, and shops, raising the population to 250,000. A prestigious retail center, the city

OPPOSITE: DAWN GREETS THE TAPPAN ZEE BRIDGE, WHICH BY DAY'S END WILL CARRY 132,000 VEHICLES BETWEEN WESTCHESTER AND ROCKLAND COUNTIES.

OVERLEAF: GOURDS AND CABBAGES SIGNAL AUTUMN AT LARCHMONT NURSERIES, A MIRROR OF THE BEAUTY OF LARCHMONT VILLAGE, ON LONG ISLAND SOUND.

Photo: © Michael Nelson/FPG International

1

Photo: © Susan Oristaglio/Esto

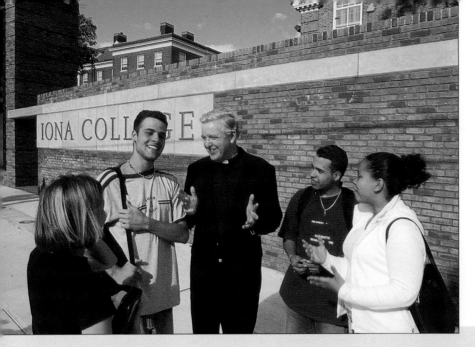

ranks fifth in the state in annual sales volume. Corporate relocation specialists note that White Plains is one of the top 10 relocation choices in the nation because of the high quality of its school system.

EVER AN EDEN

Arguably, the local site that best sums up what is happening in Westchester is Sleepy Hollow. In 2000 the village had 9,212 persons on 2.3 square miles, giving it a moderate density of 3,544. But between 1990 and 2000, its population grew by a shocking 13 percent, compared to 9.4 percent for the Big Apple.

Westchester County has always grown for the same reasons Sleepy Hollow grew: the Eden it forever presents to the surrounding area.

ABOVE: STUDENTS SHARE A LIVELY EXCHANGE WITH ONE OF THEIR PROFESSORS OUTSIDE THE MAIN GATE OF IONA COLLEGE IN NEW ROCHELLE. OPPOSITE: NATURAL LIGHT ENHANCES A COLLECTION OF ORIGINAL ART IN THE GALLERY AT LYNDHURST, A 67-ACRE ESTATE BUILT IN 1838 FOR FORMER NEW YORK CITY MAYOR WILLIAM PAULDING. THE GOTHIC REVIVAL MANSION IN TARRYTOWN IS NOW A NATIONAL TRUST HISTORIC SITE.

DORENE HOROWITZ SENIOR VICE PRESIDENT/DISTRICT EXECUTIVE, WESTCHESTER COUNTY, HSBC BANK USA

The success of HSBC Bank USA in the Westchester business community stems from our commitment to meeting the needs of our local markets. With 27 branches throughout Westchester and Putnam Counties, we serve a wide array of business organizations. From offering basic banking services to sole proprietors to leveraging our global resources for multinational companies, HSBC is committed to delivering products and services that help our customers to effectively manage and grow their businesses. And, most importantly, it is our dedicated, experienced, knowledgeable professionals that put HSBC's resources to work for the benefit of our customers every day. All our professionals have a single goal: satisfying our customers' financial needs.

DAVID A. CAPUTO PRESIDENT, PACE UNIVERSITY

Pace University understands that being a good neighbor means becoming part of a community and a partner in its development. Since opening our first location in Westchester County in 1962, Pace has been an involved neighbor in this region.

The Pace Law School established its Judicial Institute in White Plains. The institute will train judges and lawyers and significantly enhance the New York State court system.

Pace's Environmental Litigation Clinic works to safeguard the most significant bodies of water in the region, from the Adirondacks to Long Island Sound.

Such concepts of service learning at Pace enrich both its curriculum and the communities it serves.

Photo: © Peter Finger/Courtesy, Iona College

Photo: © SuperStock, Inc.

ROLF CLASSON PRESIDENT, BAYER DIAGNOSTICS

Bayer Diagnostics is committed to giving back to the communities in which we do business by supporting nonprofit organizations that contribute to enhancing life for people in the community. Bayer Diagnostics achieves this by providing both community grants and employee volunteer grants through the Bayer Foundation. The foundation focuses giving in the areas of civic and community programs, education, and health care. Employee volunteer grants help support our employees who are making a positive impact in their own home communities on their own time. Our outreach to the community is just one more way Bayer Diagnostics lives our mission to make a positive difference to human health.

Bayer ⊕
Diagnostics

Making a positive
difference to
human health

www.bayerdiag.com

FRANK E. WEBERS, PRESIDENT & CEO, COLLINS BROTHERS MOVING CORPORATION

Westchester County, with its balanced mix of business and residential areas, offers to its residents and local businesses an opportunity to grow and prosper. And Collins Brothers takes pride in being headquartered in Larchmont, having served the needs of its customers from this Westchester location since 1910. Dedicated to providing professional, efficient moving and storage services to both residential and commercial customers, Collins Brothers handles local, long distance, and international relocations. Because it is important to give something back to the community that has served us so well, Collins Brothers supports local charities, such as Swim Across America's local swim events to fight cancer and Westchester's Cancer Support Team, as well as an array of local sports teams and police events.

CP54007LOGO.HR

Photo: © Scott Barrow Inc./stock Barrow

Residents of the Bronx, the only part of New York City contiguous to Westchester, marvel at the large homes and greenery of Westchester County and the sense they feel when visiting of going out of the city and into the country.

As befits an Eden, the county is also part of America's literary and cultural heritage. In 1819 Washington Irving published a tale called "The Legend of Sleepy Hollow," and children's stories have never been the same. It began gently enough, talking about "Tarry Town" and, not far away, "a little valley . . . which is one of the quietest places in the whole world. A small brook glides through it, with just murmur enough to lull one to repose; and the occasional whistle of a quail or tapping of a woodpecker is almost the only sound that ever breaks in upon the uniform tranquility."

Soon, however, paradise is transformed. The author introduces one of the oddest of literature's oddballs, a gangling, superstitious schoolteacher with the marvelously outlandish name of Ichabod Crane, whose romantic endeavors quickly get sidetracked by one of the great, horrific figures of American writing, a headless horseman.

Many writers and entertainers were inspired by Westchester County. George M. Cohan, for example—the original Yankee Doodle Dandy—

SUNLIGHT GLINTS OFF BOATS DOCKED IN THE MARINA AT CROTON-ON-HUDSON, WHERE THE VIEWS NEVER QUIT. THE PROTECTED DEEPWATER PORT IS MINUTES AWAY FROM THE CROTON-HARMON TRAIN STATION, WHERE METRO-NORTH AND AMTRAK PROVIDE EASY ACCESS.

sang that New Rochelle was only "45 minutes from Broadway" in his vaudeville hit of the same name. Years later, that town became the home of television's Rob and Laura Petrie in the 1960s *Dick Van Dyke Show* and the setting for E. L. Doctorow's 1975 novel, *Ragtime*, which was made into a movie and a Broadway play.

One of the most famous fictional residents of Westchester County arrived in 1939. With storm clouds threatening Europe, novelist/playwright Thornton Wilder relieved cares with a delightful piece called *The Merchant of Yonkers*, in which the matchmaker Ms. Levi helps an affluent businessman in that bustling borough find the right gal. The play went through several variations until in the 1960s it opened as a musical on Broadway, and all America was saying "Hello, Dolly!"

One other local spot made it into the movies. In the sleepy little town of Ossining, there's a place known to every fan of Jimmy Cagney gangster flicks simply as Sing Sing—the state penitentiary.

FORTUITOUS HERITAGE

In all fairness, Sing Sing is hardly a typical spot in Westchester County. But Rye is. The oldest city in the county, Rye was pioneered by settlers from England in 1660. Soon after landing, they signed a treaty with the

STEPHEN J. SWEENY, PH.D. PRESIDENT, THE COLLEGE OF NEW ROCHELLE
In a world that demands that college graduates be technology-oriented, is there still a relevant place for liberal arts graduates—women and men who have degrees rooted in philosophy, literature, art, poetry, and religion?

At The College of New Rochelle, we believe that a liberal arts degree is just what college graduates need. While the term "liberal arts" might seem old fashioned, it signifies the depth and breadth of our curriculum, which provides students with the skills, knowledge, and confidence to earn a living and to be a positive influence in the world. A liberal arts education at CNR means the full development of the human person and wisdom to last a lifetime.

Wisdom for life.
The College of New Rochelle

fifth of that space—a full 20 percent—is reserved for recreation, parks, forests. The city has a protected harbor on Long Island Sound; quiet, lapping brooks where the sun glints off flowing waters; and tree-lined streets. John Jay, the first chief justice of the United States Supreme Court, is buried in Rye. A historic museum housed in an inn on the old stagecoach route dates back to the 1700s; the Rye Arts Center is likewise housed

Mohegan Indians guaranteeing peace and opening the door to business opportunities. Five years later they named the spot not after bread or whiskey, but to honor ancestors in Rye, England.

Today Rye is an inviting city of almost 15,000, with every kind of amenity. Its residents work in several large and more than 200 small companies within the urban boundaries, but they also commute throughout the county and to places as widespread as New York City, Long Island, New Jersey, and Connecticut. Two-thirds of the households live in single-family homes that cover approximately three-fifth's of Rye's six square miles. Another

ABOVE: THE WINDOW DISPLAY OF AN ANTIQUE STORE IN LARCHMONT HONORS BOTH PAST AND PRESENT. WITH A DECORATIVE ARTS INDUSTRY GOING BACK TO THE DAYS OF HENRY HUDSON, WESTCHESTER COUNTY IS AWASH IN ANTIQUES—THEY CAN BE FOUND IN NOOKS AND CRANNIES, BARNS, EMPORIUMS, AND EVEN ON THE WEB. OPPOSITE: IT'S 1929, AND ALL EYES ARE ON A CHAMPIONSHIP GOLFER AT APAWAMIS COUNTRY CLUB IN RYE. TODAY MORE THAN 10 SCENIC GREENS SPRAWL ACROSS THE COUNTY, FROM YONKERS TO NORTH SALEM.

in a building constructed in 1788. Forty-seven acres of woodlands were preserved in 1959 as the Rye Nature Center, and a 127-acre country club opened recently. Rye even has its own amusement park, Rye Playland.

Rye is just one small part of Westchester County, but that is exactly the point. If a single term sums up this special place, it is "opportunity." For business. For lifestyles. For whatever makes the heart soar.

THOMAS A. RENYI CHAIRMAN AND CEO, THE BANK OF NEW YORK

Westchester has been our home for over 30 years. Our continued support and involvement in economic development projects, annual fund-raisers, community building programs and nonprofit organizations have proven our dedication throughout the years. The Bank of New York, the nation's oldest bank, has an extensive presence in the Westchester community, as well as the resources and expertise to provide quality services to our clients.

The company provides a complete range of banking and other financial services to corporations and individuals worldwide through its core businesses: securities servicing and global payment services, corporate banking, BNY asset management and private client services, retail banking, and global market services. For more information, visit our Web site at www.bankofny.com.

THE BANK OF NEW YORK

Photo: © Susan Oristaglio/Esto

Photo: © Bettmann/CORBIS

FRANS VAN DER MINNE PRESIDENT AND CEO, HEINEKEN USA

Westchester County is a very special place. Its quality of life, diversity, and proximity to exciting places and activities make it one of the great locations to live in America. It is also a great place to do business. That is why Heineken USA is headquartered in the county, in White Plains. Our location is well situated for access to a highly qualified workforce and to important resources, and it is close to many of our biggest consumer markets. We also have a lot in common with the county. We are the world's most international beer company. Westchester has a wealth of diversity from all over the world. We both have Dutch heritage.

We both are committed to good citizenship and individual responsibility. Westchester County is a great place to work and to live.

Chapter 2

Creating Tradition

THE EVENTS AND IDEAS THAT SHAPED THE COUNTY

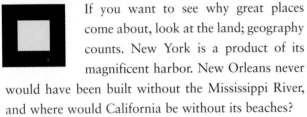 If you want to see why great places come about, look at the land; geography counts. New York is a product of its magnificent harbor. New Orleans never would have been built without the Mississippi River, and where would California be without its beaches?

Like these special parts of America, Westchester County was blessed with fortuitous terrain. The Hudson River, one of the early nation's most important arteries, rolls by on the west, while the east gets caressed by the waves of the Long Island Sound. Three smaller rivers, furthermore, bisect this space—the Croton, Bronx, and Saw Mill—giving access to what, in colonial days, was a more important form of transportation than the heavy carts used on land.

It was these waterways that brought the first European settlers. They, in turn, encountered the indigenous residents, members of the Algonquin and Mohegan tribes. These peoples lived a peaceful existence, hunting and fishing, growing corn and pumpkins, harvesting oysters and other shellfish from the abundance the rivers seemed to eternally provide.

Then, in 1609, Henry Hudson arrived. An English explorer commissioned by the Dutch, Hudson took his soon-to-be-eponymous waterway as far north as Albany and sent messages back about all his local stops, one of which was at Yonkers.

It wasn't called that back then, of course. But one of the earliest landlords in the area was a Dutch aristocrat named Adrian Van der Donck, who was also the first lawyer in the New Netherlands colony. Van der Donck's nickname was Donk Herr—"young gentleman"—and soon his property became known as Donk Herr's land. This became shortened and tightened to "the Younckers," and eventually, simply Yonkers.

What drew men like Van der Donck was opportunity, rooted in the very soil of Westchester County. In 1638 William Kieft, head of the New Netherlands colony, took a pioneering step to attain growth and prosperity. Even though this was an age of global competition, Kieft knew the key to local success and issued a directive that in his settlement, anyone could own land, even foreigners. This brought, for example, English settlers, some seeking economic benefits, others religious freedom. More important, however, the values behind Kieft's directive—that tolerance was important, that old views shouldn't stand in the way of new enterprises—became part of the fabric of Westchester County. In 1664 all of New Netherlands became British property (causing a name change to honor the Duke of York); soon after, the colony welcomed the French Huguenots, Protestants fleeing persecution in their homeland. This group built its own settlement in the local area, naming it after the French port La Rochelle.

OPPOSITE: ENGLISH NAVIGATOR HENRY HUDSON, WORKING FOR THE DUTCH, DISCOVERED THE RIVER THAT BECAME ONE OF EARLY AMERICA'S MOST IMPORTANT, THE EPONYMOUS HUDSON. OVERLEAF: AN 1856 ENGRAVING DEPICTS INDIGENOUS AMERICANS WITH HUDSON'S MEN AS THE EXPLORER SAILS DOWN THE RIVER.

Photo: © Hulton|Archive

Photo: © Bettmann/CORBIS

Photo: © Lee Snider/CORBIS

DREAMS OF FREEDOM

In 1775 more changes occurred. A rumble was heard around the world that still echoes today. Men like Jefferson and Adams, Washington and Hamilton, came up with the idea that citizens had a right to freedom, even to choose their own leaders. It was, as they say, a revolution. On July 11, 1776, at the County Courthouse in White Plains (now the armory), orators delivered the first public reading in New York State of the Declaration of Independence.

These were hard years for the county, as much of the revolution was fought on local soil. In the war's early years, the Continental Army suffered a number of defeats and had to retreat inland, coming to rest, bloody and exhausted, in upper Westchester; General Washington's headquarters, in fact, were at Continental Village, near Peekskill. Raiders burned houses, stealing local produce, and young men went to war and never came back; the postrevolution census was 1,000 less than the population that had first marched off to fight for freedom.

That was Westchester's most important contribution to the struggle, but there was also the work of three native sons who arrested a Major John André on September 23, 1780. These lads from Tarrytown had picked up one of the most famous and important spies in all of American history. André carried papers indicting a top-ranking American officer who had been planning to

ABOVE: IN AN 1825 ETCHING, THE FIRST BARGES FROM BUFFALO ARRIVE IN NEW YORK HARBOR VIA THE NEWLY OPENED ERIE CANAL. BELOW: ROBERT FULTON'S STEAMBOAT PLANS (TOP) REVOLUTIONIZED WATER TRAVEL. OPPOSITE: THE JACOB PURDY HOUSE SERVED AS GEORGE WASHINGTON'S TEMPORARY WAR HEADQUARTERS.

turn over West Point, the most important fort on the Hudson, to the British; he even had drawings of the installation's defense layout hidden in his boot. But when the Tarrytown troopers arrested him the jig was up, and the name of André's coconspirator, Benedict Arnold, became a cliché, a standard term for traitors to this day.

Washington's forces triumphed eventually, and a new country, followed by a remarkable constitution, came into being. The nation's first census, in 1790, showed just how far Westchester had come—the population had grown to 24,000—and hinted at what was about to happen.

Another revolution, that of transportation, brought the county to new heights. In 1807 Robert Fulton transformed the way the world's citizens got around when he invented the first successful steamboat; that year the *Clermont* took its first trip, up the Hudson to Albany. In 1825 the Erie Canal opened, linking the harbor in New York City to the Great Lakes via the Hudson River and turning New York, New York, into the most important port in the nation. Soon factories and factory workers appeared in all of the river towns. Iron stoves and agricultural implements were made in Port Chester and Peekskill; bricks were shaped and fired in Croton; marble was quarried in Tuckahoe and Ossining.

Westchester was thriving. Between 1845 and 1855 the population increased by 33,000. In 1851 John Stevens,

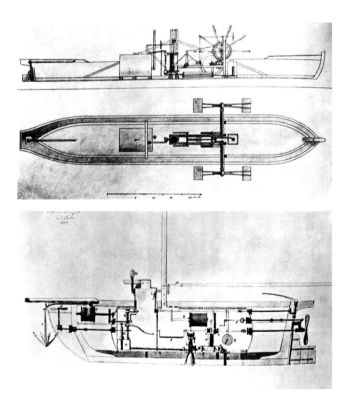

Photos: Top, © Hulton|Archive; bottom, © Bettmann/CORBIS

ABOVE: CHEMIST LEO BAEKELAND OF YONKERS INVENTED THE FIRST TRUE PLASTIC. BELOW: YONKERS RESIDENT EDWIN ARMSTRONG (SHOWN WITH HIS RADIO RECEIVER) DISCOVERED THE PRINCIPLE THAT MADE RADIO BROADCASTING POSSIBLE, THEN INVENTED THE FM BAND. OPPOSITE: THE MILLS OF ALEXANDER SMITH & SONS CARPET CO. CONTRIBUTED TO THE COUNTY'S 19TH-CENTURY BOOM.

a skilled workman in New York City, bought five farms in Westchester, totaling 369 acres, on which he built houses for working families. For these people, this meant finally being part of the American dream. The tract of land became Mount Vernon, eventually one of the county's largest cities.

FAST TRACK TO INNOVATION

Westchester now entered one of its greatest boom eras, a period that would extend past the Civil War and into the new century. This was the nation's great burst of industrialization, and the county played a big role. In 1854, for example, Rudolph Eickemeyer revolutionized the hat industry by patenting a blocking and shaping machine, and within a few years the county was the nation's leading center in the production of chapeaus.

Other industries, like rubber making and sugar processing, followed, with new enterprises coming fast and furious from Westchester residents. The Standard Oilcloth Company began production in Buchanan, while Zinsser Chemical and Hastings Pavement located in Hastings. Some of these new factories were giants—such as Yonkers-based Otis Elevator and the Alexander Smith Carpet Company, which pioneered in the development of new types of looms—while some were

unlikely successes, like the Lord & Burnham Greenhouse Manufacturing Company in Irvington. Yonkers, meanwhile, put up the first street lighting system in the country in 1861.

Edwin Armstrong invented the FM radio and Leo Baekeland built a box for it. After inventing one of the first commercial photographic printing papers, Baekeland created the original synthetic plastic, which he called Bakelite. In 1914 Western Electric used it to make telephone receivers, the predecessor of models we still have on our desk. Before Bakelite, radios were housed in steel or wood boxes, turning them into fine furniture with enormously high prices compared to the plastic-encased ones that followed. Bakelite made this product, and the later televisions as well, available to a broad audience in a host of colors and shapes no machinist or woodworker had ever dreamed of.

All these businesses needed workers, and Westchester's population soared, matching the robustness of the growing nation it was so much a part of. Between 1865 and 1920, for example, the county grew from 100,000 to 350,000 people, roughly matching

Photos: Top, courtesy, Union Carbide Plastics Company, Division of Union Carbide Corp.; bottom, Bettmann/CORBIS

MOQUETTE MILLS.

WEAVING MILLS.

SPINNING AND PRINT MILLS.

ALEXANDER SMITH & SONS CARPET CO.
YONKERS, N. Y.

Photo: Courtesy, Westchester County Historical Society

2

Anna Jones, who became the first African American woman to join the New York State Bar.

The county enlisted in other national causes as well, such as World War II. The famous Norden Bomb Sight was a White Plains product. General Motors' Westchester factories made airplane parts, while the Alexander Smith carpet mills cranked out tents and uniforms. In 1941 Terrytoons Studio, in New Rochelle, created one of the great war heroes, a cartoon character that would go on to delight children throughout the 1940s and 1950s: Mighty Mouse. That year, for the very first time, he sang out in his baritone voice "Here I come to save the day. . . ."

After the war, the county blossomed. The Bronx River Parkway, America's first limited-access road, opened in 1925 to rave reviews for its convenience and beauty. By the 1930s it had been joined by the Saw Mill River Parkway, the Hutchinson River Parkway, and the Taconic State Parkway. These roads guaranteed that Westchester County would soar. GIs were coming home and starting families. With the baby boom, big cities like New York soon got crowded. Families needed space, and good transportation meant increased opportunities. Westchester beckoned, as it does today, with its solid homes, good schools, and employment and entrepreneurial opportunities.

Fortune 500 companies also saw what Westchester had to offer, beginning a process of moving corporate headquarters to the county that continues to this day. The modern Westchester County was now emerging, a good place to do business as well as enjoy the quality of life. Galleries appeared in increasing numbers, and in 1965 the county created the Westchester Arts Council to promote all art forms in the local area. Among the most notable of those is Summerfare, a two-month-long

America's expansion from about 38 million to 105 million in the same period.

ABOVE: CARRIE CHAPMAN CATT, ONE OF THE KEY THINKERS OF THE SUFFRAGE MOVEMENT, TAKES PART IN A NEW YORK CITY PARADE. AFTER HELPING WIN WOMEN THE RIGHT TO VOTE, THE LEAGUE OF WOMEN VOTERS FOUNDER SPENT HER LATER YEARS IN NEW ROCHELLE. OPPOSITE: PLANS FOR THE WESTCHESTER ARTS COUNCIL'S ARTS EXCHANGE GALLERY ARE IN THE WORKS, PROMISING A SUPERB CULTURAL EXPERIENCE.

GOING THE MILE

The county also got involved in the causes of the day, standing up for progress and international freedom. Women's suffrage had a strong following in Westchester, and by 1915, 20,000 local women were enrolled in 102 suffrage clubs. In 1928 Carrie Chapman Catt, one of the foremost leaders of this movement and in many ways its leading thinker, moved to New Rochelle; there she joined

festival put on by the State University of New York's Purchase College that provides world-class musical, theatrical, and dance performances.

All the county's efforts have paid off. Today, just under one million in population, Westchester County stands solidly on its roots, ready for whatever excitement the future may bring.

Photo: © Bettmann/CORBIS

Photo: Courtesy, Sullivan Architecture

PROPOSED
WESTCHESTER ARTS COUNCIL
CHASE BUILDING   WHITE PLAINS NY

2

Chapter 3

The Essential Tool

Brain power is standard fare in Westchester County, and it's nurtured by a superb school network at every level. In 1998, for example, Westchester's high school students earned an average SAT score of 1014, 16 points higher than the mean for New York State.

Still another measure of academic success is the state's Regents examinations, competency exams prepared by the state's Board of Regents. In 1996 Westchester County students scored an average grade of 91.3 percent in English, compared to 81.6 percent for the state as a whole. The gap narrowed in U.S. history a tad, as the county racked up 90.7 percent to the state's 82 percent. But the county came roaring back in math and the sciences, with the cumulative average for three levels of math exams coming out to 85.1 percent for Westchester, as opposed to 75.3 percent for the state. Again, in biology, Westchester achieved an average student grade of 83 percent to the state's 69.6 percent.

Among the other barometers of academic success is the fact that in 1999, almost 90 percent of high school graduates went on to attend institutions of higher education, with some districts reporting almost universal attainment of this goal.

These results do not happen by themselves; they are the product of Westchester County's commitment to education. Median expenditure per student is almost $13,000 a year, and the median pupil-to-teacher ratio is an astonishing 13 to 1, accenting the intense amount of personal instruction that is so crucial to success. But that's why 30 county schools were recognized by the U.S. Department of Education as National Schools of Excellence. And when, in March 2000, the county announced that Cablevision Lightpath would build a high-speed fiber-optic network linking schools, libraries, hospitals, and municipalities, Vice President Al Gore named Westchester the first Access America community in the nation, calling it "a true model for others to follow."

The Board of Cooperative Educational Services (BOCES) helps those students who wish to follow a vocational career path, including adults seeking to improve their status at work or in the community. More than 7,000 people attend BOCES' day, evening, and weekend classes in 20 career programs, from special education to information systems. The county also maintains a number of Special Act Districts, which offer education and therapeutic care to students between the ages of five and 21 who have had difficulties in more conventional programs.

These programs are augmented by the more than 120 private schools in the county, many of them nationally known, such as the Rye Country Day School (which has a student-to-teacher ratio of 8 to 1), Iona Prep in

OPPOSITE: BRESCIA HALL, WITH ITS GOTHIC ARCHITECTURE, TYPIFIES THE BUILDINGS AT THE COLLEGE OF NEW ROCHELLE, ONE OF WESTCHESTER COUNTY'S MOST HIGHLY REGARDED INSTITUTIONS OF HIGHER LEARNING.

Photo: © Peter Finger/Courtesy, The College of New Rochelle

3

Photo: Courtesy, New York Medical College

New Rochelle, or any of a number of foreign language–oriented schools, like the French American School in Larchmont, the German School of New York in White Plains, or Keio Academy of New York in Purchase.

HONOR ROLL

Westchester County's institutions of higher learning not only provide remarkable opportunities for local students, they draw some of the nation's brightest young minds, students who often take up residence in the area after graduation.

There are 28 colleges and universities just within the county where students can earn an advanced degree, and the diversity of programs reflects a vast array of opportunities. Take, for example, internationally known Sarah Lawrence College in Bronxville. Founded in 1926, the school holds that the essential foundation for clear reasoning is exposure to the great traditions of intellectual, artistic, and scientific thought. It advances these goals by encouraging a bond between educator and student. Students help design their own program, and instruction takes place via small seminars and tutorials. The student-to-faculty ratio is 6 to 1. Besides undergraduate programs, Sarah Lawrence offers master's degrees in eight fields, from women's history to theater to genetics. In 2000 the editors of *The Best College for You* (copublished by *Time* magazine and the *Princeton Review*) named Sarah Lawrence as Liberal Arts College of the Year.

ABOVE: SARAH LAWRENCE COLLEGE FOCUSES ON INTELLECTUAL, ARTISTIC, AND SCIENTIFIC THOUGHT. BELOW: NURSES PLEDGE ALLEGIANCE DURING COMMENCEMENT AT THE COCHRAN SCHOOL OF NURSING. OPPOSITE: NEW YORK MEDICAL COLLEGE STUDENTS CHAT ON THE WAY TO CLASS. OVERLEAF: IONA COLLEGE'S HAGAN SCHOOL OF BUSINESS IS AMONG THE NEW YORK METRO AREA'S MOST INNOVATIVE.

The College of New Rochelle, another highly regarded institution, was founded in 1904 as a liberal arts school for women. Its school of arts and sciences maintains that tradition, while the school of nursing, graduate school, and school of new resources are all coeducational. That last institution is a leader in adult education, offering liberal arts degrees via both traditional classroom work and independent study options. Many of its students continue on and earn advanced degrees from prestigious universities such as Harvard, Yale, Princeton, and Columbia.

Other Westchester schools excel in the professional disciplines. Iona College in New Rochelle, for example, is especially strong in business and accounting, as is Pace University, which offers graduate business degrees at its graduate center and the juris doctor at its law school, both in White Plains. Long Island University also maintains a graduate program on the campus of the State University of New York (SUNY) at Purchase, while Fordham University offers graduate programs in business, education, and social work from its facilities on the Marymount College campus in Tarrytown. In the fields of medicine and health sciences, Westchester County is the home of New York Medical College in Valhalla (since 1860), the Cochran School of Nursing in Yonkers, and the Dorothea Hopfer School of Nursing at the Mount Vernon Hospital.

Photos: Top, © Susan Oristaglio/Esto; bottom, courtesy, Cochran School of Nursing at St. John's Riverside Hospital

3

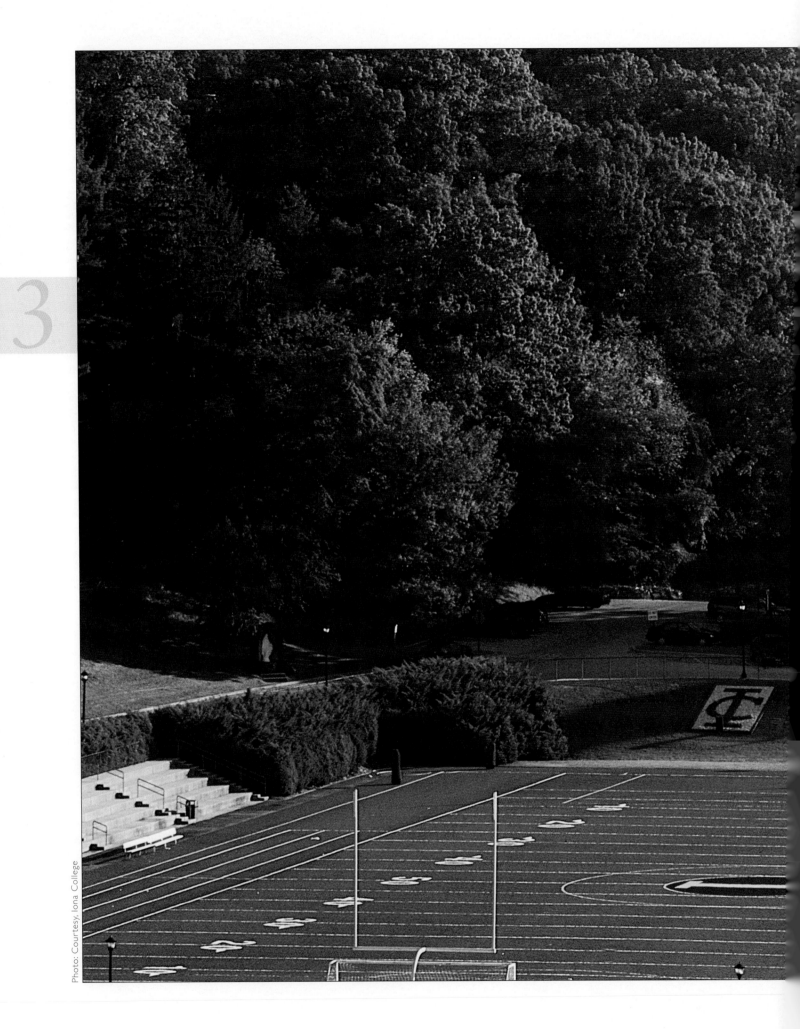

Photo: Courtesy, Iona College

Purchase (Purchase College). It was founded in 1967 on a 500-acre farm formerly owned by Revolutionary War hero Thomas Thomas.

In its 2000 listings, *U.S. News & World Report* ranked the college as one of the top two public liberal arts colleges in the North. Two-thirds of the college's 4,000 students take the traditional liberal arts and sciences curriculum, but unlike most schools of this sort, a full third is enrolled in the conservatories of dance, music, and theater arts and film and in the school of art and design.

Purchase College is an exceptional place to study the arts, and not just because it is situated only half an hour from New York City. The catalog of the conservatory of dance speaks for all of the college's arts programs when it states, "This is not a program for dabblers. Commitment, intensity, and exceptional talent are essential qualities for all successful Conservatory applicants."

Those who make it into the arts programs study under faculty drawn from the ranks of the most accomplished professionals in the nation. Students perform in and have access to facilities that are among the best, from the Gunner Birkerts–designed dance building, the first in the nation to be constructed solely for that art form, to the world-renowned performing arts center, where more than 600 student and professional performances are put on each year.

This is a school that turns out winners. Two alumni, artist Fred Wilson and environmental scientist Carl Safina, were awarded MacArthur Fellowships in 1999 and 2000 respectively, while another alumnus, playwright Donald Margulies, won a Pulitzer Prize in 2000. Other school veterans are now household names, like Stanley Tucci, Wesley Snipes, Parker Posey, and even Edie Falco, who won an Emmy Award for her outstanding work on TV's HBO hit series *The Sopranos*.

STEPPING STONE TO SUCCESS

One of the most distinctive institutions in the area is Westchester Community College (WCC), located on 218 acres in Valhalla. The student body can comprise as many as 20,000 students per semester, including continuing education attendees. It offers three types of associate degrees—in arts for those continuing on to four-year schools in the liberal arts; in science for those going on in business, math, or health; and in applied science for individuals seeking immediate employment—in 40

Berkeley College, on the other hand, specializes in business at the associate and baccalaureate levels as well as providing certificate programs. Its five locations in the New York/New Jersey region include a campus at White Plains. Bachelor's degrees are awarded not only in business management but in such fields as e-business, Internet Web technologies, and network management; associate degree programs cover these areas and more, such as fashion marketing and management and international business. The school also offers the opportunity to become a Microsoft Certified Systems Engineer (MCSE), one of the top credentials in information technology.

DABBLERS NEED NOT APPLY

Adding to Westchester's array of excellent schools is an outstanding public institution, the SUNY campus at

Photo: Courtesy, Westchester Community College/© G. Steve Jordan

RYE COUNTRY DAY SCHOOL

different fields. In addition, it offers certificate programs in another 17 career fields. More than 94 percent of the faculty have master's or doctorate degrees; teachers and staff have earned more SUNY Chancellors Awards for Excellence than any community college in the system.

The school embraces the needs of the community, offering associate of applied science (A.A.S.) degree programs in, for example, computer information systems, automotive engineering, medical laboratory technology, and office and law office technologies. It is also at the cutting edge of new ideas as a charter member of the SUNY Learning Network, a system whereby students attend classes via their computer.

In March 2001, WCC opened a biotechnology and health care training center in Ossining as part of the county's $50 million capital improvement project to

Photo: © Susan Oristaglio/Esto

ABOVE: THE DAY'S STILL YOUNG AS MIDDLE SCHOOL STUDENTS EMERGE FROM RYE COUNTRY DAY SCHOOL, ONE OF THE NATION'S PREMIER PRE-K THROUGH 12 PRIVATE SCHOOLS. OPPOSITE: AN INSTRUCTOR AT WESTCHESTER COMMUNITY COLLEGE GUIDES THIS BUDDING ARTIST IN REFINING HER TECHNIQUE.

develop educational resources in crucial growth areas. The new facility has three classrooms; two computer rooms; labs for biology, computers, and health skills; plus office space. The biology lab is the setting for WCC's first course in biotechnology. The health skills lab has simulated hospital and home settings along with the latest CPR and medical technician emergency gear.

Some of the finest and most diverse educational institutions in the world are situated in Westchester County, making it possible to pursue practically any kind of dream.

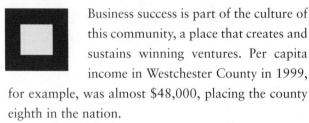

The Marketplace

Chapter 4

HIGHLIGHTS OF A HOT ECONOMY

Business success is part of the culture of this community, a place that creates and sustains winning ventures. Per capita income in Westchester County in 1999, for example, was almost $48,000, placing the county eighth in the nation.

Westchester is part of a major metropolitan region, just 35 minutes from New York City and 15 from either New Jersey or Connecticut. This provides local businesses with a wealth of markets and potential employees that cannot be achieved in more isolated places. And when income is measured just for counties that are part of metropolitan areas, Westchester ranks third in the nation.

Superlatives crop up in the county like wildflowers, even concerning buildings. An office tower like Westchester One, for example, in White Plains, designed by Copland Novak & Israel, is not only one of the tallest buildings in the county, at 23 stories and 850,000 square feet it would hold that title in most medium-sized cities as well. If, on the other hand, companies are looking for a wider horizontal footprint, 2000 Westchester Avenue in Harrison, designed by Skidmore, Owings & Merrill, has almost 700,000 square feet but is just four stories tall.

September 2000 unemployment was 3.3 percent, the lowest since 1988. A representative of J.P. Morgan Chase & Co. recently declared that despite the bad news from many of the nation's tech giants, the picture for Westchester and the Bronx remained upbeat, with no major slowdowns in the county at all; in fact 80 percent of Westchester-based companies were looking for employees.

This robustness is in part the result of a highly diversified economy. Many representatives of the Fortune 500's top tier are long-term residents of the county, and at the same time, a vibrant community of small entrepreneurial operations is generating ideas, wealth, and jobs. While the county may be home to IBM and PepsiCo, the number of businesses with under 100 employees grew by 13 percent between 1994 and 1999, resulting in 23,000 new jobs locally. There are also roughly 10,000 minority-owned firms and 28,000 women-owned businesses.

It is this mix of major corporate players and low-scale, high-energy entrepreneurial ventures that makes Westchester County so vibrant.

LEADERSHIP WITH A CONSCIENCE

The county has been one of the nation's leading centers for corporate headquarters since shortly after World War II. By the early 1950s, large corporations were looking to move beyond their urban settings. They sought room to build out, not just up, and good roads that could accommodate traffic without becoming clogged. They wanted open space and fresh air, and

OPPOSITE: AN INSURANCE AGENT USES EVERY MOMENT AS HE WAITS FOR THE TRAIN, THOUGH HE'LL BE HOME IN 15 MINUTES. THE COUNTY'S ACCESSIBILITY ENABLES IT TO DRAW EMPLOYEES FROM A NUMBER OF NEARBY METRO AREAS.

Photo: © CORBIS

4

Photo: © Susan Oristaglio/Esto

Photo: © Digital Stock

perhaps a lake view to sooth nerves in an increasingly competitive environment. It also wouldn't hurt if costs were lower.

Westchester County met all these needs and still does. Its bucolic settings encourage thought and leadership. Its traffic flow is rapid transit compared to the crawl that exists in so many big cities. And even now, rents are 55 percent lower than comparable space in Manhattan; operating costs and taxes, a remarkable 68 percent lower.

The corporate surge began in 1953, when General Foods (now Kraft Foods) moved its headquarters out of Manhattan to the fertile fields just north of the city line. There was no question that this company was a giant, with some of the most famous brand names in the country, from Maxwell House (coffee) and Birds-Eye (frozen foods) to Jell-O (desserts) and Post (cereals). The move to Westchester must have gone down right, for the years following were innovative: in 1957 the company brought out Tang instant breakfast drink, which would be carried on the early manned space flights; in 1965, Shake 'n Bake coating mix; and in 1966, Cool Whip topping.

General Foods' original headquarters in Rye Brook is typical of the kind of

General Foods was the pioneer, but many other giants followed. Today there are four Fortune 500 companies headquartered in Westchester and another seven have corporate offices there. Add to this the synergy of being in the largest and most financially powerful metropolitan area in the nation, with 44 Fortune 500 headquarters less than an hour's drive away, and it becomes clear that the opportunities for leadership are unparalleled.

What kind of companies move to the Westchester County area today? One example of a local Fortune 500 firm is PepsiCo, whose world headquarters is situated on 144 acres of land in Purchase. The company employs 135,000 people around the globe; its 2000

ABOVE: "SLOW" ISN'T PART OF THE COUNTY MIND-SET, AS A LAWYER ON HIS WAY TO COURT ILLUSTRATES. OPPOSITE: FROM THIS OFFICE TOWER IN WHITE PLAINS TO SPRAWLING OFFICE PARKS IN BUCOLIC SETTINGS, WESTCHESTER HAS SPACE GALORE.

contribution large firms like this have made to the quality of life in Westchester County. To enhance the natural beauty of the wetlands site the company had chosen, the architects (Kevin Roche, John Dinkeloo & Associates) built a large lake as part of the open landscape, adding to the county's amenities.

revenues were over $25 billion. PepsiCo's many brands include not only the flagship cola but also Tropicana (fruit juices), Gatorade (sports drink), Aunt Jemima (pancake mixes and syrups), and Frito-Lay (snacks), the latter commanding close to 60 percent of the U.S. snack chip market.

PepsiCo's seven-building complex, spread over 10 acres, was designed by Edward Durrell Stone. The property includes the Donald M. Kendall Sculpture Gardens, originally created by landscape designer Russell Page, which showcases world-class, 20th-century art in lush garden settings. Among the masters represented are Rodin, Moore, Calder, Giacometti, and Oldenburg. This special resource is, of course, open to the public.

ROOM TO GROW, IN STYLE

Giant firms like these are constantly growing, and Westchester County can easily accommodate the changes. Heineken USA just expanded its headquarters in White Plains, as did Starwood Hotels & Resorts Worldwide, another Fortune 500 firm. This is an international powerhouse, with more than 738 hostelries worldwide, including the Sheraton,

Instead, the company stayed in Westchester. In spring 2000, Starwood announced plans to move to a 203,000-square-foot site in White Plains, a location large enough to accommodate all the existing administrative branches as well as another 300 employees from the company's outlying sites. Furthermore, Starwood estimates that its headquarters workforce will double within five years.

One of the best known corporate headquarters in Westchester County belongs to IBM, based in Armonk. The company's latest structure is a three-story,

BELOW: TARRYTOWN CORPORATE CENTER SEES A ROBUST MIX OF TENANTS, SOON TO INCLUDE QUAKER FOODS & BEVERAGES. OPPOSITE: AN ALEXANDER CALDER SCULPTURE GRACES THE PEPSICO HEADQUARTERS IN PURCHASE.

Z-shaped building designed by Kohn Pedersen Fox Associates on a 432-acre site at the top of a tree-filled ravine. The views are magnificent, as is the scope of the building: 300,000 square feet with space for 600 employees.

Both interior and exterior designs are state of the art. Take, for example, the main videoconferencing room, with its magnificent high, sloped ceiling and floor-to-ceiling windows. The setting proved a challenge, for while the room provided a balance between the best that humanity and nature could create, it also built in a formidable wash of backlight.

Westin, Four Points, and new W chains, as well as a dozen top-of-the-line vacation ownership resorts. Worldwide, Starwood employs approximately 120,000 people.

Throughout the nineties Starwood's headquarters in White Plains grew, until the company needed several locations in Westchester. Consolidation was the obvious next step, and given Starwood's clout, it had lots of suitors, including the state of Connecticut.

Lighting designers Kugler Tillotson Associates met the challenge by creating a custom fixture, a 13-foot, six-inch-diameter circular light that hovers over the center of the room. The ring of light provides four separately dimmable modes of illumination, creating a variety of working environments through its water-white glass panels. The result is not only a functional masterpiece but, as interior architects Swanke Hayden Connell noted, an expression of steel and glass

Photo: © Susan Oristaglio/Esto

Photo: Courtesy, PepsiCo

Photo: Courtesy, IBM

completely appropriate to the place, like a beautiful piece of jewelry.

OUTSTANDING MIX

Westchester County is as nurturing to start-ups as it is to giants. That's why there are so many small firms making exciting breakthroughs in fields like biotechnology.

The Landmark at Eastview in Tarrytown is a good example of what is happening locally. The privately owned multitenant science park is located in the center of the county, in the Saw Mill River Valley. There are 740,000 square feet of space in five buildings and a host of amenities, including tennis and basketball courts, jogging trails, free shuttle service to the Metro-North station—and an on-site owner. Not surprisingly, Landmark at Eastview is doing well. Tenants include biotech companies Progenics Pharmaceuticals, Regeneron Pharmaceuticals, Cerami Consulting, and Emisphere Technologies; R&D companies Ciba Specialty Chemicals, in materials science, and Praxair, in industrial gases and equipment; and telecommunications firm Cap Gemini America.

Landmark is not alone in its success. In 1997, no less a figure than Governor George Pataki announced that several corporate players in the Ardsley Park Science and Technology Center in Greenburgh were about to expand, and that Finnish firm Cultor Food Science (now Danisco Cultor) had just leased 100,000 square feet in Ardsley. Cultor proceeded to invest $23 million in new labs and equipment and move 170 jobs from operations in Groton, Connecticut, and Manhattan; the average salary for those jobs was $70,000.

At about the same time, Purdue Pharma LP, headquartered in Stamford, bought a 105,000-square-foot lab building at Ardsley for a new R&D facility and put almost $15 million in capital improvements into the site. Soon after, it bought a second building in the park and

has continued to expand. The company now employs 200 individuals at Ardsley and plans to double its workforce by 2004.

The spirit of partnership is alive and well in the county. Economic development and government officials work hand-in-hand with the private sector to develop high-growth industries and good jobs. Whether a company has already become a corporate empire or is just starting to build one, the county stands ready to support every element in this remarkable mix.

BELOW: NEW YORK GOV. GEORGE PATAKI, SHOWN SPEAKING TO THE PRESS AFTER A RECENT MEETING AT THE WHITE HOUSE, TAKES AN ACTIVE INTEREST IN WESTCHESTER BUSINESS. OPPOSITE: SITUATED ON 432 ACRES ATOP A WOODED RAVINE IN ARMONK, THE IBM HEADQUARTERS IS CONSIDERED A FUNCTIONAL MASTERPIECE.

Photo: © Reuters NewMedia Inc./CORBIS

Chapter 5

Ordinary Miracles

ADVANCES IN HEALTH CARE AND PHARMACEUTICALS

■ If Westchester County is in sound health, there's a good reason. It is home to some of the nation's top biotechnology research firms as well as a number of the best hospitals available anywhere.

More than 8,000 people work in biotechnology in the county, nearly 20 percent of total New York State employees in this sector. These individuals work for companies like Progenics Pharmaceuticals in Tarrytown, pioneering in the fight to find drugs that will initiate an immune response in the body. This kind of disease killer is aimed at a range of potentially lethal organisms such as HIV or malignant melanoma, and it provides a potent weapon for researchers—and soon, possibly, doctors as well: the company's antigen-based cancer vaccine is the first of its kind to begin Phase III clinical trials.

Tarrytown is also home to Regeneron Pharmaceuticals, dedicated to developing therapeutic drugs that deal with serious medical conditions such as cancer-related disorders, inflammatory conditions like rheumatoid arthritis, and allergies, asthma, and obesity. One of its most important new drugs, Axokine, treats obesity.

Geritrex, a Mount Vernon company founded by pharmacists more than 15 years ago, is one of the nation's top producers of pharmaceutical products for hospitals and health care institutions, specializing in lines that deal with infection control, wound care, skin and personal care, and bathing and whirlpool therapy.

WORLD-CLASS CARE

Westchester's pharmaceutical companies are backed by an extensive network of health care facilities. Some of these are giants, such as the Scarsdale-based National Home Health Care Corporation, whose subsidiary Allen Health Care Services provides nurses, home care aides, and homemakers throughout the larger New York metropolitan area.

The Sound Shore Medical Center of Westchester is another giant. It began back in 1892 with four nurses and eight beds in a single wooden house in New Rochelle. Sound Shore now has 465 beds, 1,000 staff members, and 700 doctors; it treats more than 80,000 individuals each year. It also has the distinction of being the largest private teaching hospital in the county (affiliated with New York Medical College) and features the first hospital-centered training program in the United States in acupuncture and oriental medicine, working with the Mercy College graduate program in this field.

Stories like this are only part of the landscape of health care innovation in Westchester County. Other institutions stand out at least as much, if not more. Take Westchester Medical Center (WMC) in Valhalla, for example, which works on the leading edge of medical research and delivery of services.

OPPOSITE: CARESSING THEIR NEWBORN, PARENTS REFLECT ON THE MIRACLE OF BIRTH. FACILITIES SUCH AS THE HUDSON VALLEY HOSPITAL WOMEN'S PAVILION FOR BIRTHING HELP MAKE THE PROCESS ONE OF UNPARALLELED JOY.

Photo: © ER Productions/CORBIS

5

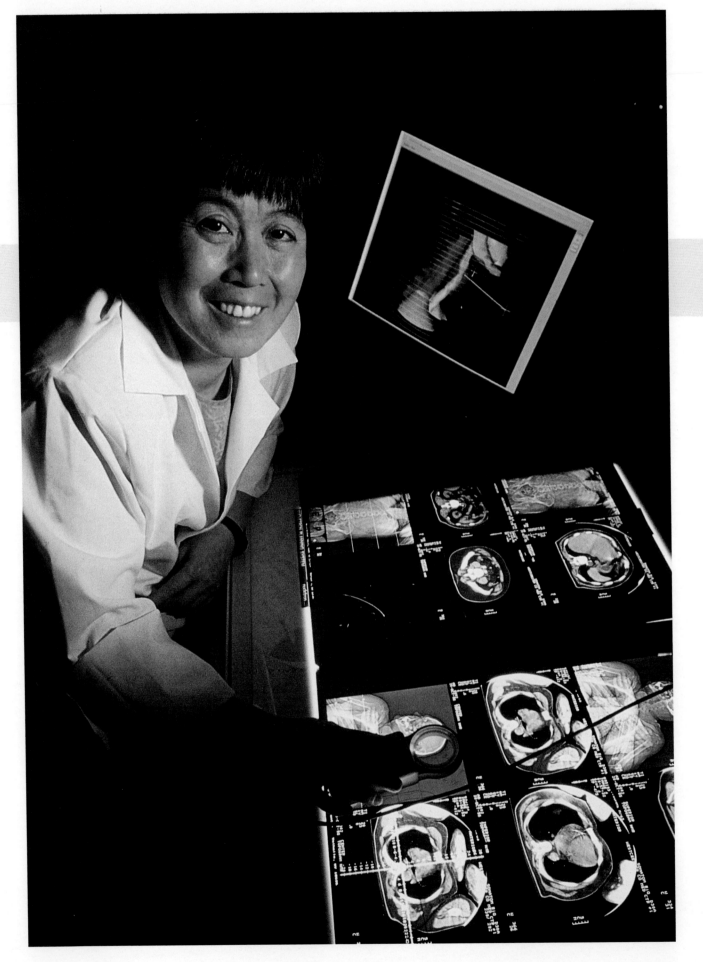

Photo: Courtesy, Westchester Medical Center

Photos: Top, © Digital Stock; bottom, courtesy, Marketing Department, Hudson Valley Hospital Center

WMC houses the largest kidney transplant program in the state and the only liver transplant program in the region. In 1999 it successfully conducted 116 kidney and 15 liver transplants from all over the upstate region as well as New York City and even Connecticut and Pennsylvania. That year, too, WMC performed the first pancreas and joint pancreas/kidney transplants ever conducted in the region. In addition, Westchester Medical Center has America's fifth largest corneal transplant program for children. The medical center is currently gearing up for its new state-approved heart transplant program.

WMC also contains the George E. Reed Heart Center, one of the top 10 in the state for cardiac surgery and cardiac catheterization (particularly impressive considering that the competition includes world-class facilities in New York City plus top medical schools like the one at Cornell University in Ithaca). The heart center also maintains a state-of-the-art diagnostic center that guarantees one of the highest rates of recovery of any hospital in the state. Recent statistics show that Reed performs over 1,000 cardiothoracic surgeries a year, almost 8,000 catheterizations, and almost 50,000 noninvasive cardiology procedures. As a teaching hospital for New York Medical College, furthermore, it participates in the latest experiments on procedures and drug therapies, keeping it at the top of a rapidly changing field that is altering how medicine is performed.

Also at WMC is the Zalmen A. Arlin Cancer Institute, which uses procedures, medicine, and

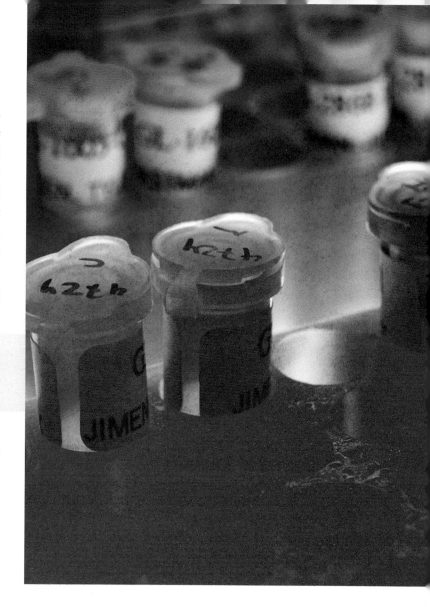

ABOVE: DNA SAMPLES AWAIT RESEARCH AT ONE OF THE REGION'S TOP BIOTECH FIRMS. BELOW: ON-THE-SPOT RESULTS OF A BLOOD SUGAR SCREENING HELP THIS TECHNICIAN IDENTIFY POTENTIAL PROBLEMS. OPPOSITE: A RADIOLOGIST AT WMC'S IMAGING CENTER HAS ACCESS TO THE BEST TECHNOLOGY AVAILABLE.

technology such as stem cell transplants long before they become available to the general public. While the center does thousands of bone marrow transplants, it has pioneered in matched unrelated marrow and cord blood transplants, vastly expanding the scope of this kind of procedure.

Westchester Medical's neuroscience center tackles brain tumors, brain attack, epilepsy, aneurysms, movement disorders such as Parkinson's, complex neuromuscular disorders, and trauma to the head and spine, as well as specializing in knifeless stereotactic radiosurgery, wherein problems deep within the brain not only can be treated without surgery but can be observed for analysis long before intervention is begun.

In a related program, WMC's Behavioral Health Center treats patients of all age groups suffering from behavioral, emotional, psychiatric, or drug- or

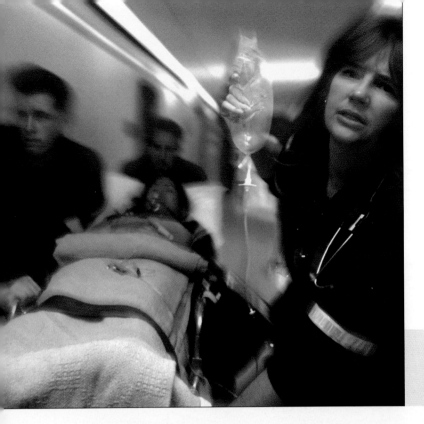

means a lot of lives saved, many measured in ounces rather than pounds.

SPECIALIZING IN INNOVATION

WMC is one of a host of advanced medical facilities in a county that boasts 23 hospitals within its borders. The Hudson Valley Hospital Center in Cortlandt Manor, for example, pioneered in establishing the midwifery profession at hospitals in the region. Over a decade ago, Dr. Theodore Beck, then chairman of the hospital's obstetrics and gynecology department, took the lead in developing not only a cadre of trained midwives but also one of the finest birthing facilities in the region.

ABOVE: MEDICAL WORKERS RUSH A PATIENT TO THE EMERGENCY ROOM OF A LOCAL HOSPITAL, WHERE EXPERTS ARE ON DUTY 24/7. BELOW: REGENERON PHARMACEUTICALS TECHNICIANS DISCUSS RESULTS OF A NEW DRUG WITH A VOLUNTEER.

alcohol-related problems. For youth requiring long-term care, it even has its own school. The center maintains a psychiatric emergency room and mobile crisis intervention team, making it one of only 15 comprehensive psychiatric emergency facilities in the state.

STAT Flight is another of WMC's rapid response facilities. The 24/7 air and ground medical response unit provides emergency helicopter and land service to a 5,000-square-mile area. Patients are taken to WMC's Level 1 trauma center, the only facility in the region with this designation.

Other WMC facilities include the Enrico "Hank" Longo Burn Center, a self-contained unit (to minimize the risk of infection), and the Westchester Institute for Human Development, one of only several dozen university-affiliated training and care programs in the United States for those with developmental disabilities such as mental retardation, cerebral palsy, spina bifida, autism, cleft lip and palate, and learning and communication disorders.

Little ones require unique programs, ranging from the most advanced technology to plenty of hugs. Children's Hospital at WMC has the region's only pediatric intensive care unit and its highest-level neonatal intensive care unit, plus its only pediatric open-heart and cardiac catheterization unit, performing more than 2,500 pediatric surgeries a year. This

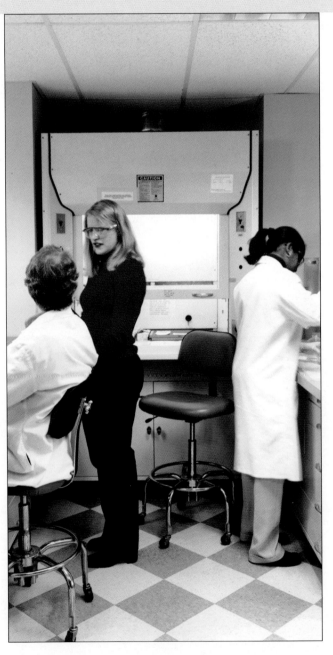

Photos: Top, © Paul Kuroda/SuperStock, Inc.; bottom, © Horacio/Courtesy, Regeneron Pharmaceuticals, Inc.

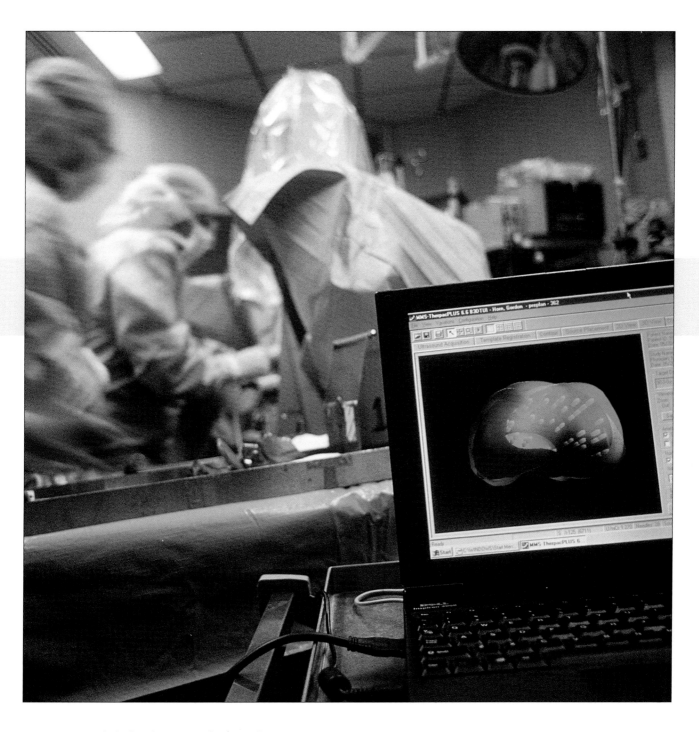

Photo: Courtesy, Westchester Medical Center

To accomplish this, he initiated a $1 million campaign to refurbish what would become the Women's Pavilion for Birthing. Dr. Beck, a large, jovial man who served the hospital for 30 years and delivered 10,000 babies, began by contributing $100,000 of his own money.

The result is a top-notch facility with 13 private, deluxe postpartum rooms, each with its own bath, and an advanced nursery unit. Every one of the five labor/delivery/recovery rooms has its own whirlpool tub, an option for labor and delivery.

Some of the top health organizations in Westchester County are smaller, with more focused missions.

WMC SURGEONS PERFORM A RADIOACTIVE SEED IMPLANTATION FOR A PROSTATE CANCER PATIENT, WHOSE INFORMATION APPEARS ON THE COMPUTER SCREEN. THE CENTER OFFERS THE MOST COMPREHENSIVE SURGICAL OPTIONS IN THE REGION.

St. Vincent's Hospital and Medical Center of New York, for example, in Harrison, is considered one of the best psychiatric facilities on the East Coast. It maintains an around-the-clock emergency facility with bilingual staff. Blythedale Children's Hospital in Valhalla has, for over a century, been treating children regardless of their ability to pay. The hospital handles primarily serious medical conditions such as injuries to the spinal cord, cancer,

On the box: KEEP IN UPRIGHT POSITION / HUMAN ORGA... / FO... / TRAN... / NEW YORK HOSPITAL... / HAN... / TRANSPLANT

LOOKING TO THE FUTURE

The county has big plans for the biotech and health care fields. Local officials have been lobbying the state to provide $20 million to create the Biotechnology and Life Sciences Research Center, which would be located on 60 vacant acres in Valhalla on the Grasslands biomed campus that already houses part of Westchester Medical Center and the American Health Foundation.

Some organizations are not even waiting for this development.

New York–Presbyterian Hospital, for example, plans to develop a new 380,000 square-foot, two-building biomedical facility on its existing 214-acre campus in White Plains. The plans put aside 80,000 square feet for a center for advanced proton therapy, a procedure that uses a proton beam accelerator to destroy cancerous tumors. Only New York–Presbyterian's Westchester site can accommodate the sheer size of this project, which includes a half-acre footprint plus a 35-foot-tall structure weighing 470 tons. At the present time, only one such facility dedicated to treating patients exists in the nation, in Loma Linda, California.

This massive development will cost $200 million, some of which will come from the state and federal governments; planners project that it will take four years to build and will provide employment for 900 individuals at all skill levels.

birth defects, and pulmonary-related disorders. Through the inpatient and day care hospital, Blythedale treats more than 200 children a day.

Westchester County also has branches of some of the top medical establishments in the United States, such as the Memorial Sloan-Kettering Cancer Center in Sleepy Hollow and, in White Plains, the Westchester Division of New York–Presbyterian, the University Hospitals of Columbia and Cornell; and Lighthouse International, a world leader in vision rehabilitation.

ABOVE: SPEED IS OF THE ESSENCE AS AN ARRIVING ORGAN IS USHERED TO THE TRANSPLANT CENTER AT WESTCHESTER MEDICAL CENTER. THE CENTER'S NEW HEART TRANSPLANT PROGRAM WILL SWING INTO OPERATION IN FALL 2002. OPPOSITE: A PATIENT CHATS WITH A NURSE'S ASSISTANT IN THE LOBBY AFTER A PROCEDURE AT THE VIRGINIA FESJIAN AMBULATORY SURGERY PAVILION AT SOUND SHORE MEDICAL CENTER.

Thus, the future looks bright for the health sciences sector in Westchester County. Health care services are top-notch and getting better all the time, and research and development firms are flourishing. With the beginnings of a biotechnology cluster already in place, the sector promises a vibrant, state-of-the-art tomorrow.

Photo: Courtesy, Westchester Medical Center

5

Photo: © Joe Vericker/PHOTOBUREAU, Inc./Courtesy, Sound Shore Medical Center of Westchester

Chapter 6

Going Places

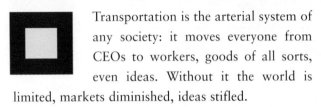

Transportation is the arterial system of any society: it moves everyone from CEOs to workers, goods of all sorts, even ideas. Without it the world is limited, markets diminished, ideas stifled.

Westchester County is in the middle of the busy Northeast Corridor, and its connections to the rest of this region are long and solid. Interstate 87 becomes the New York State Thruway, linking the county south to the Big Apple, north to places like Montreal, and—by connecting to the I-90—west to upstate cities like Albany and Buffalo, and beyond them, the Great Lakes region all the way to Chicago. Interstate 95— the New England Thruway—provides access to Connecticut, Massachusetts, and on up to Maine. Traversing the county along east-west lines is the Cross Westchester Expressway, providing easy connections to New Jersey. This road is "corporate central" in Westchester; with so many company head-quarters located along the route, locals call it the Platinum Mile. All told, there are over 3,200 miles of state and local highways serving the needs of just this one county.

And some of these are beauties. New York State pioneered in the development of not just freeways but also parkways, limited-access roads running through majestic woodlands, roads that would help preserve this scenic heritage and make it accessible to all. The Taconic State Parkway, for example, which links Westchester and Albany in the north, is arguably the loveliest in the nation, its gently curving roads providing a lush, verdant vista. Its companion, the Bronx River Parkway, was the first limited-access highway ever constructed in America, and it was soon joined by cousins like the Saw Mill River Parkway and the Hutchinson River Parkway.

FAST TRACK

Even with all these routes, getting into the metropolis just south of Westchester can still be a daunting problem; nowhere else in the nation does traffic move more slowly than in Manhattan, or so it seems.

Thus, there are alternatives to the car, superb ones. Westchester County boasts the MTA Metro-North Railroad, the second largest commuter system in the United States, making 240,000 trips each weekday and carrying 71.9 million riders a year. This system consists of three main lines running through the county, with a total of 120 stations available, guaranteeing that park-and-ride is never more than a short hop away. During rush hour, this service beats auto transport hands down; instead of being stuck at an unbudging, unending tollbooth line, Metro-North passengers move. It takes only 37 minutes, for example, to go from White Plains, the county seat, to Grand Central Station in the heart of the city itself.

OPPOSITE: A SECTION OF THE GLOBE PAINTED ON THE TAIL OF A CONTINENTAL AIRLINES JET IS REMINISCENT OF THE WORLD-CLASS ADDITIONS RECENTLY MADE AT WESTCHESTER COUNTY AIRPORT, WHICH NOW SERVES MORE THAN 12 CITIES.

Photo: © Scott Barrow Inc./stock Barrow

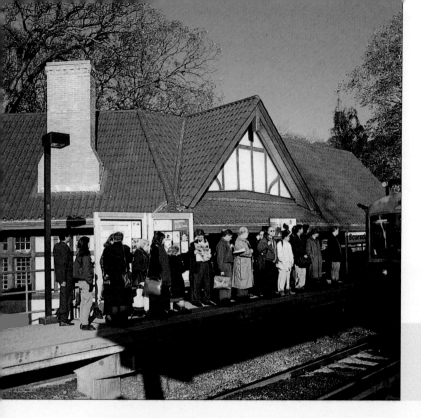

ABOVE: PASSENGERS AT SCARSDALE STATION PREPARE TO BOARD AN ARRIVING METRO-NORTH TRAIN, PART OF THE COUNTY'S OUTSTANDING COMMUTER RAIL SYSTEM. BELOW: AIR TRANSPORT LINKS WESTCHESTER COUNTY TO THE NATION.

In addition to being efficient, Metro-North offers a bonus that has to be seen to be believed. The Hudson line runs along the glorious Hudson River, and the views in every season, from the blaze of fall color to the majesty of white snow, have inspired artists since the early 1800s—particularly the painters of the Hudson River School.

This massive system is in good physical and financial shape, as well. The railroad's 2000–04 capital program calls for $1.3 billion in expenditures, of which 39 percent ($521 million) will pay for new rolling stock and 22 percent ($295 million) for new or upgraded passenger stations. Yonkers, for example, is in the process of getting a $34 million reworking of its facility in conjunction with a waterfront revitalization by the county and local municipality. Plans are also under way for a new, $20 million Metro-North station at Yankee Stadium, in the Bronx, which would link Westchester County directly to those hallowed grounds.

There are other ground transportation services as well connecting Westchester County to the region. New Rochelle, for example, has a station on Amtrak's Boston-Washington line, with express Metroliner service available.

Inside the county, the Bee-Line Bus System, which has a fleet of more than 300 buses, carries an average of 100,000 people a day to their destinations and back.

FLYING HIGH

Some trips take the traveler farther, of course, and these require air travel. Westchester has its own airport, the eponymous Westchester County Airport (HPN), a growing, bustling place. In recent years the county added a $22 million, 44,000-square-foot terminal and operations center, as well as a three-level, 1,200-car garage. The airlines took notice, and now major carriers like American, Continental, Northwest, and United whisk passengers from HPN to more than a dozen cities, 10 of them (including Boston, Chicago, Atlanta, Washington, Detroit, and Minneapolis) via nonstop service. Not surprisingly, the airport also is home base for some of the largest fleets of corporate aircraft and helicopters in the world. Overall, HPN now enplanes and deplanes over one million passengers a year, generating more than $600 million annually for the Westchester County economy.

County officials understand the value of transportation. They helped bring Atlas Air, one of the largest air cargo carriers in the world, to this business mecca along the Hudson. Founded in 1992, Atlas is the world's largest outsourcer of Boeing 747-400 and 747-200 aircraft. When the giants of the passenger airline industry need to rapidly expand their cargo capacity on a short-term basis, they turn to Atlas, eliminating the need for vast, prolonged capital expenditures or personnel costs.

Instead Atlas maintains for their use the world's largest fleet of 747 freighter aircraft. The company is

Photos: © Susan Oristaglio/Esto; bottom, © Digital Stock

now the third largest carrier on the planet, its tonnage exceeded only by Federal Express and United Parcel Service. Its service reaches 101 cities in 46 countries, and the list is growing, all of its services being used by existing airlines to augment their own operations at the cheapest price possible. Atlas can do this because its operating margin is generally among the highest of any of the world's airlines, and most years the carrier is ranked by trade journals as the most financially fit in the world.

In 1999 Atlas Air, with its global reach and global vision, found itself needing more space than its Golden, Colorado, site could offer. With revenues up a stunning 42 percent, the company urgently required an alternative location that would allow it to keep growing. It chose Westchester County.

ABOVE: THE BRONX RIVER PARKWAY WAS THE NATION'S FIRST LIMITED-ACCESS ROAD TO RUN THROUGH MAJESTIC WOODLANDS. OVERLEAF: SCENIC TACONIC PARKWAY CONNECTS WESTCHESTER COUNTY WITH ALBANY, IN THE NORTH.

The site the corporation picked was in one of the county's premier office parks, the Texaco headquarters complex in the Purchase section of Harrison. On June 5, 2000, Atlas Air took occupancy of 120,000 square feet. With this one step, the company not only brought together its disparate operations from all over the map but also added 450 employees to the county's expanding workforce.

In Westchester County, the sky is never the limit. Travel is easy and convenient, linking business, cargo, or people to wherever the dream or necessity may lead—in the fastest way possible.

6

Photo: Scott Barrow Inc./stock Barrow

Chapter 7

Spreading the Word

INFORMATION TECHNOLOGY AND THE MEDIA

If, in the past, knowledge helped create power, it has now become one of the most important tools in the world of business. Westchester County not only uses it as a basis for communications, it specializes in creating new forms of information technology and then marketing the ideas and products resulting from these innovations.

PINNACLE OF TECHNOLOGY

Zeroes and ones may not look like much, but more and more, we live in a world where they are used to represent our words, our ideas, our images, our creativity. The digital revolution has remade the world of business, and Westchester County has taken a leadership role in this unprecedented wave of change.

More than 1,700 companies in the county design computer systems, and 85 manufacture computer and electronic products. Data flows countywide over a 400-mile fiber-optic loop that links business to government and to the world with impressive speed and power. No matter where one works in Westchester, for example, he or she will find 100 percent digital switching with full capability for the transmission of voice and video, and even video teleconferencing and dial-up video conferencing.

A system like this comes about because all the major players are interested in making high tech work. Thus local leaders, led by Art Zuckerman of Armascan Technology Corporation in New Rochelle,

created the Westchester Information Technology Cluster (WITC), which brought together the resources of business, government, and education.

This pioneering effort works almost exclusively by means of new age technology—with a few tips of the hat to the past. When, for example, it was discovered that each year 1,000 students graduated from local schools with degrees in information technology but often went to jobs elsewhere, the cluster created Cyberside Chats. The name came from President Franklin Roosevelt's reassuring talks during the depression, and the goal here was also positive: to make sure those students knew about possibilities within the county so they would have a full range of choices when they made employment decisions.

In response, 52 local businesses and seven local institutions of higher learning initially signed up with the cluster. Graduating seniors could now plug into the chats, where academic counselors took a look at their records, matched their skills and training to the needs of local companies, and arranged an introduction. The process has led to hundreds of successful connections, the product of lots of hard work, foresight, and sheer tenacity on the part of Westchester's movers and shakers.

Since this beginning, WITC has expanded and grown. At present it has over 200 members, 58 percent of which are involved in various aspects of the computer

OPPOSITE: MICROWAVE COMMUNICATIONS TOWERS LIKE THIS, WHICH TRANSMIT AND RECEIVE SIGNALS FROM WIRELESS AND ELECTRONIC MEDIA, ARE ON THE RISE IN THE COUNTY. THE INCREASED COMPETITION BRINGS LOWER RATES.

Photo: © CORBIS Stock Market/Lester Lefkowitz

industry, 18 percent in creating and managing software, and 27 percent in providing services and products to Internet firms. They cooperate in hiring, sharing leads, acquiring discounts on purchases, developing relationships with schools, plus gaining publicity and sharing Web sites and databases.

What type of companies get involved in this kind of positive environment? The answers are limited only by the sheer creative output of the human mind.

Greenwich Technology Partners (GTP), for example, is a leading network infrastructure consulting and engineering firm. GTP specializes in designing, building, and managing complex networks using advanced Internet protocol, electro/optical, and other technologies and can handle everything from systems engineering to computer security. The company, which had been operating for some time in Stamford, Connecticut, relocated in White Plains on a 30,000-square-foot site.

Metromedia Fiber Network (MFN) leads the pack when it comes to creating high-bandwidth optical

ABOVE: THANKS TO THE COUNTY'S SOPHISTICATED INFRASTRUCTURE, THESE BUSINESS PARTNERS CONSULT VIA VIDEOCONFERENCE. OPPOSITE: A YOUNG RADIO BROADCASTER ENJOYS THE JOB—AND HE DIDN'T HAVE TO GO SOUTH TO GET IT.

Internet infrastructures. The company is constructing networks in 51 North American and 16 European cities. Based in White Plains, MFN recently moved its corporate offices to an 80,000-square-foot site.

Other local companies are expanding the notion of what can be done using new technology. Westchester Technologies, located in Peekskill, manufactures high-precision micro-optical components for the telecommunications, fiber-optics, and other industries. The company opened its manufacturing facilities in 1986 and now makes everything from raw glass to the most subtle finished elements for highly sophisticated systems.

HIGH RATINGS

Westchester County provides numerous ways to get the word out, whether it's to reach potential customers,

Photo: © Wayne Eastep/Stone

spread the news, or entertain. Besides all the radio, television, and cable stations that originate in New York City and are available just north of the city line, the county hosts five FM radio stations of its own (WFAS, WZZN, WXPS, WLNA, and WVOX), plus four AM stations (WVIP, WFAS, WLNA, and WVOX). General cable service is provided by Cablevision of Westchester, which also built the county's giant fiber-optic loop. In addition to the usual array of cable channels, Cablevision also runs Westchester 12 News, an all-news channel serving the county in particular and the Hudson River Valley in general.

One indication of this station's quality is its editorial director, Paul Loewenwarter, who served for 18 years as a producer of the acclaimed *60 Minutes* program on CBS and in 1986 left to start his own production company. Paul Loewenwarter Associates produced one of the initial television documentaries on the AIDS crisis, *The National AIDS Awareness Test*, which was broadcast on 120 stations, and, with ABC News corre-spondent Hugh Downs, put on *The National Cholesterol Test*. Working with industry, he created the award-winning five-part series *Thriving on Chaos* with

management expert Tom Peters and numerous other top-quality programs.

Print media are also flourishing in Westchester County. Of the major newspapers serving the county as a whole, the most important is the daily *Journal News,* published by the Gannett Company. The paper's four editions serve northern Westchester/Putnam Counties, central Westchester, southern Westchester, and Rockland County. The *Journal News* Web site, furthermore, provides what may be the greatest community service of them all: a real-time camera showing traffic conditions at crucial sites on the freeways, updated every two seconds.

A host of weeklies, such as the *North County News,* the *Scarsdale Inquirer,* the *Rye Chronicle,* and the *White Plains Watch,* address individual communities.

Westchester provides a number of special interest newspapers as well, including such titles as the *Hudson Valley Black Press,* a weekly out of Newburgh; *El Aguila del Hudson Valley,* a monthly published in Beacon; the Westchester edition of *The Jewish Week,* which, with a five-region circulation of 90,000 house-holds, is the largest Jewish newspaper in America; and

Photo: © David Seed Photography/FPG International

ABOVE: FOR THIS YOUNG WOMAN, ANY TIME'S THE RIGHT TIME TO CATCH UP ON FEATURES IN THE MONTHLY *EL AGUILA DEL HUDSON VALLEY*, A U.S. NEWSWIRE PICK FOR THE TOP **300** HISPANIC MEDIA PACKAGES. BELOW: PRESSES ROLL ON ONE OF THE COUNTY'S NUMEROUS MAGAZINES. OPPOSITE: PRIOR TO THE DAY'S BROADCASTING, AN ENGINEER FINE-TUNES EQUIPMENT AT A LOCAL CABLE **TV** STUDIO.

Women's News, covering issues relating to the family and the home.

Other publications reflect the upscale style of life in the county and one of the most important and basic interests of that life: business. *Westchester Spotlight,* an elegant monthly magazine out of Elmsford, features articles on the good life, from dining, real estate, and home design to health, education, and business. The Healthcare Research Group, out of New Rochelle, covers national issues in its publications *Managed Healthcare Market Report, Seizing the eHealth Market Opportunity,* and *eHealth Insider.* County business trends are covered by the weekly *Westchester County Business Journal,* which also publishes the invaluable reference work *The Book of Business Lists;* and *Westchester Commerce,* a monthly business publication put out by the Westchester Chamber of Commerce.

Then there is the monthly *Westchester WAG,* a paper that takes its title from the dictionary definition of the term *wag:* "a person given to droll or mischievous

humor." This publication covers the county's movers and shakers as well as its galas, bashes, and benefits every month in an entirely appropriate fashion. In the paper's own words, the *WAG* is "always fun, always wicked."

The county provides an atmosphere in which news and creativity are valued, whether the medium is old or new. While the county has, for example, 326 companies that deal in broadcasting and communications, 471 involved with the motion picture or video format, and 73 that engage in some aspect of sound recording, this is also the kind of place that supports 83 book-stores and 68 newsstands.

Every businessperson knows that knowledge is the future. With its strong roots in high technology, information management, and media services, Westchester County is rocketing into that world of tomorrow.

Photos: Top. © Ulises Gonzáles/El Aguila; bottom, © Digital Stock

Photo: © CORBIS Stock Market/Roger Ball

Chapter 8

Superb Support

With Westchester County serving as home base for so many businesses, it follows that its business and professional services are tops. From banking to energy, real estate to law, a myriad of companies serves the needs of this dynamic community.

Every business needs money, and both corporate officers and entrepreneurs usually turn to their banker first. In many ways, the Westchester pioneer in this area was William Butcher, who was particularly active in the fifties and sixties, but whose legacy is still potent.

Born and raised in Brooklyn, Butcher began his career in Cincinnati working for the Central Trust Company, where he developed his style of doing business: personal *personified*. If he believed in something, he became involved at every level. When, for example, the lifelong baseball devotee found that his company had acquired the Cincinnati Redlegs, he saw to it that the team hired first-rate executives. To increase attendance, Butcher introduced night games to major league baseball and hired Red Barber as the team's announcer, starting the career of one of America's greatest sports figures.

Another of Butcher's passions was the game of checkers, which he had learned from local citizens on Manhattan's Lower East Side, many of them living on the Bowery near the facility his father headed for homeless boys. When the New York papers announced in 1957 that Butcher had risen to the top

of Westchester County Trust, one of his old companions from those days, now a top corporate lawyer, called and made a healthy deposit. For William Butcher, personal ties always counted.

Though the players have changed, Butcher's spirit still pervades the banking community in Westchester County. Today there are 18 commercial banks with 261 local branches, plus 15 savings and loans with another 41 offices. The list of commercial banks includes international giants like the JPMorgan Chase and Citibank, and even The Bank of New York. There are also branches of Fleet Bank, Union State Bank, HSBC Bank USA, Key Bank, and Banco Popular North America. Top savings institutions like Dime Savings Bank of New York and Emigrant Savings Bank serve Westchester too, as do financial services companies such as American Express and Merrill Lynch.

These firms still believe in serving their clients and seek out new ways to do so, just as William Butcher did. Fleet Bank in Westchester, for example, took note that by the end of the last decade, New York State had 600,000 women-owned businesses, representing 37 percent of the total of all firms in the state. The bank set up the Women Entrepreneurs' Connection to serve as an advocate and resource for these innovators. The Connection is a means not only to educate

OPPOSITE: U.S. CURRENCY: IT'S THE BOTTOM LINE, AND A BEVY OF BANKS, FINANCIAL SERVICES COMPANIES, ACCOUNTANTS, AND BOOKKEEPERS, ALONG WITH LOCAL GOVERNMENT, PROVIDE THE EXPERTISE TO MAKE IT GROW.

Photo: © Myron/Stone

women entrepreneurs to the array of services banks offer but also to provide entrée to a host of other business institutions via a whole new set of networking opportunities.

GOING BY THE NUMBERS

Getting money is one thing; keeping track of it is another. Westchester County has over 2,300 companies involved in accounting, bookkeeping, payroll services, and tax returns. That list is headed by firms like Marden, Harrison & Kreuter, which has 54 CPAs available throughout the county, and O'Connor Davies Munns & Dobbins, LLP, with 40; both are located in White Plains.

RSM McGladrey is also typical of the firms that serve Westchester County. Specializing in medium-sized

DIME SAVINGS BANK IS ONE OF THE COUNTY'S MANY FINANCIAL INSTITUTIONS THAT STILL BELIEVES IN SERVING THE CLIENT, OFFERING, FOR EXAMPLE, AN ARRAY OF PROGRAMS AND OPPORTUNITIES GEARED TO OPENING ECONOMIC DOORS.

companies, McGladrey provides accounting, tax, and consulting assistance for local businesses. When needs arise that extend beyond the immediate setting, McGladrey's 100 offices nationwide assist the client. Beyond this range, the company offers the services of the McGladrey Network, 70 independent accounting and consulting firms that are linked with the parent company by cooperative agreement. If, on the other hand, business ventures take a company overseas, this accounting giant is still prepared to handle financial issues through its affiliation with RSM International, one of the world's largest accounting organizations.

Photo: © Susan Oristaglio/Esto

In addition to private sector firms, the county government is a superb resource for economic development. Not the least of its accomplishments is that Westchester is the most creditworthy county in the state, with a triple A bond rating.

The county put together Team Westchester to help businesses set up shop or expand locally. It comprises representatives of programs from the county as well as from New York State, Con Edison, and local cities. These entities help with such matters as development financing, energy cost reduction, and coordinating employment programs.

Of particular importance is the Westchester County Industrial Development Agency, which helps arrange long-term financing at favorable rates as well as exemptions from sales tax for major expenditures.

IMPECCABLE JUDGMENT

People make lots of jokes about lawyers, but every good businessperson knows the truth: no firm can, or should, operate without legal support. Westchester County offers a wealth of talent in this field.

The largest firm in the county is Bleakley Platt & Schmidt LLP, based in White Plains. The firm began in 1937 when William F. Bleakley, who had been a justice in the New York State Supreme Court, put out a shingle in partnership with Livingston Platt, who had years of local experience. Members of the firm began a long tradition of involvement in local government, which

ABOVE: FEDERAL CASES ARE TRIED AT THE NEW U.S. COURTHOUSE IN WHITE PLAINS, DESIGNED BY SKIDMORE OWINGS AND MERRILL. BELOW: AN ATTORNEY CHECKS A POINT OF LAW BEFORE A CLIENT MEETING. OVERLEAF: THE FINANCIAL DISTRICT IN THE COUNTY SEAT HELPS FUEL THE REGION'S BUSINESS GROWTH.

included simultaneous federal chief judgeships held by two former partners in the late 1980s.

Today Bleakley Platt & Schmidt is a powerhouse, with 47 lawyers in the county. It maintains 12 practice groups, covering banking, corporate, environmental, health services, labor, litigation, municipal, product liability, real estate, property assessment, tax, and trust and estate law.

Another major player is Cuddy & Feder & Worby LLP, also out of White Plains. Founded in 1971, the firm began by specializing in land-use issues, handling numerous large commercial office, retail, and multi-unit residential projects. This work expanded to cover the entire gamut of real estate; much of the county's "miracle mile" of office parks along the I-287 corridor, along with a great deal of downtown White Plains' new office and shopping development, is a product of this firm.

Photos: Top, © Susan Oristaglio/Esto; bottom, © Dennis O'Clair/Stone

Photo: Financial Center in White Plains. © Susan Oristaglio/Esto

Today Cuddy & Feder & Worby has gone even further, handling regulatory approval of cellular towers, subsidized housing, and environmental issues. At the forefront of technology, the firm offers a specialty in computer and on-line law, covering everything from the licensing of software to establishing start-up firms and even advising large corporations on Internet legalities, one of the thorniest and most rapidly shifting fields of law imaginable.

POWER PACKED

Another area undergoing rapid transformation is the energy industry. In many places this changing landscape has caused consternation and shortages, but Westchester County stands on firmer ground.

The county's electrical needs are served by Consolidated Edison Company of New York, which has been doing business for 175 years. It delivers electricity to an area of about 660 square miles that includes all of New York City and most of Westchester, providing the company with three million customers who rely on it to be there when they turn the lights on each day.

Con Ed lives up to that trust by delivering approximately 50 billion kilowatt hours of power a year, a figure made possible by having plants with the capacity to generate 8.5 million kilowatts at any given time. This generating capacity, in turn,

Photo: © Digital Vision

Photo: © Digital Vision

depends on a network of 90,000 miles of underground electric cable—the largest in the world—and 35,000 more miles of wire overhead.

Con Ed also supplies natural gas to one million customers. To serve these needs, it operates 6,600 miles of gas pipes, which carry 200 million dekatherms of natural gas a year.

The utility's assets total $15 billion, and it has increased its dividends every year for the past 27 years. All this while giving customers rate reductions that will total $1 billion over a five-year period, with four-fifths of this savings going to small businesses and residential customers.

A second utility serving the area is the New York State Electric and Gas Company (NYSEG), a growing firm that provides electricity to 825,000 customers across the state and natural gas to 246,000. In 1999 the number of NYSEG electric customers was up by 4 percent; gas customers, by 9 percent—and the reason is good service. The company has the lowest customer complaint rate of any electric and gas utility in the state. There are just 1.6 calls per 100,000 customers, three

ABOVE: NATURAL GAS PLANTS LIKE THIS ONE PROVIDE COUNTY RESIDENTS WITH CLEAN ENERGY AT REASONABLE PRICES. OPPOSITE: LINEMEN WORK QUICKLY TO REPAIR HIGH-TENSION WIRES, ENSURING CONTINUED DELIVERY OF ELECTRICITY.

times better than the closest competitor. When people do call, the average wait time is under 25 seconds, and 92 percent of customers report full satisfaction with the first call, a figure that has received national recognition.

NYSEG does even more than that. The company realized that the large workforce it has out in the field every single day, reading meters and fixing lines, could be an invaluable community resource. So NYSEG organized Community Watch, turning its field work-force into a vast network of eyes and ears for police, fire, emergency, and highway services. This translates every year into lives saved and property protected.

ATTENTION GETTERS

Adding to the county's extensive list of professional services are 1,021 companies that provide advertising and related services, led by Eric Mower and Associates (EMA), the largest ad agency in the state outside of

Manhattan. The company maintains five of its six offices in upstate New York, including one in White Plains. With campaigns all over the globe, EMA employs more than 225 top professionals and bills over $130 million annually. It focuses on the fields of agribusiness, consumerism, energy, entertainment and tourism, finance, food and beverages, health care, higher education, manufacturing, and technology, serving clients ranging from the American Red Cross to DuPont Pharmaceuticals.

Another example of the talent in this sector is Delfino Marketing Communications in Valhalla. The company has more than 30 years of experience handling not only traditional public relations responsibilities but also direct mail promotions, sales presentation materials, and trade shows. Its client list includes such nationally known firms as Roche Pharmaceuticals, Brunswick Billiards, and Fleischmann's Yeast, helping it bring in nearly $2.5 million in annual revenue. FastForward Communications, another Valhalla advertising, public relations, and marketing trendsetter, has been in business 15 years. The firm sees sales of about $760,000 to $1 million a year.

In the long run, the county's ability to support business also depends on intangibles, such as the ability

ABOVE: MANY A DEAL IS SEALED AFTER A GALA DINNER IN A BREATHTAKING SETTING SUCH AS ABIGAIL KIRSCH CULINARY PRODUCTIONS' HISTORIC TAPPAN HILL MANSION, OVERLOOKING THE HUDSON RIVER IN TARRYTOWN. OPPOSITE: REPORTS ANALYZING MEDIA PLACEMENT GIVE A THUMBS-UP TO LOCAL MARKETING FIRMS.

to create trust. A setting where business relationships can be established in a positive and convivial environment can help.

Enter Abigail Kirsch Culinary Productions. Kirsch, a woman with a long line of culinary credentials, founded the firm more than 25 years ago. Based in Tarrytown, Kirsch Culinary Productions has a staff of roughly 120 full-time and 500 part-time employees and handles about 2,000 events a year.

These are the people who make an evening special. A typical menu for a gala dinner starts with hors d'oeuvres like steamed shrimp dumplings and crème fraiche caviar served with homemade waffle potato shells. Then it proceeds to an appetizer such as lobster and corn soufflé enhanced with tricolored peppers, shallots, and cilantro. After a rose champagne sorbet, the entrée arrives: beef Wellington stuffed with duck liver paté and wild mushroom duxelles. Dessert is chocolate cake with an oozing ganache center, served with vanilla bean ice cream.

With that kind of meal, what couldn't be accomplished in Westchester County?

Photo: © Yale Joel

Photo: © Eyewire, Inc.

Chapter 9

The Finer Things

TOURISM, ENTERTAINMENT, AND THE RETAIL MARKET

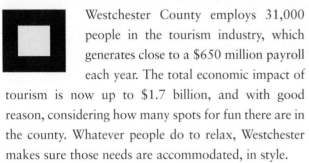 Westchester County employs 31,000 people in the tourism industry, which generates close to a $650 million payroll each year. The total economic impact of tourism is now up to $1.7 billion, and with good reason, considering how many spots for fun there are in the county. Whatever people do to relax, Westchester makes sure those needs are accommodated, in style.

Business travelers find Westchester County well prepared for their arrival with 251 establishments providing accommodations, including 108 rooming and boarding houses. Westchester has two Hilton Hotels, plus branches of the Marriott, Ramada, Hampton Inn, and Holiday Inn chains, and new branches of Extended Stay America, Comfort Inns and Suites, and Renaissance Hotels. The total inventory of rooms in the county is now over 4,000, and premier facilities like the Crowne Plaza White Plains, Rye Brook's Hilton Rye Town and Doral Arrowwood, and the Westchester Marriott in Tarrytown even have their own high-tech convention centers.

If something more is needed, there is the Westchester County Center in White Plains. A gorgeous art deco building, the center has 50,000 square feet on three levels, with seven meeting rooms and space to accommodate 300 exhibitors. Sound systems and lighting are the best available, and the kitchen can feed 2,000 people at a time.

Westchester excels at another kind of commercial center as well, the kind designed for shoppers. The county was actually one of the suburban pioneers in this kind of enterprise; originally the downtown section of cities had been the center of retail trade, but in 1934 B. Altman expanded from its famous site at 34th Street and 5th Avenue in Manhattan and opened a store in White Plains. Arnold Constable, another New York retailer, followed this lead in 1937, and after the war, Macy's and Lord & Taylor showed up, along with several other major New York City stores.

Westchester never stopped building on these early developments, and today customers flock to shopping malls like the Westchester in White Plains. Opened in 1995, this 829,000-square-foot facility is anchored by both Neiman-Marcus and Nordstrom stores, the latter commanding over 200,000 square feet alone. Upscale shops like Tiffany's, Brooks Brothers, and FAO Schwarz, nestled among the 160 various boutiques and specialty stores, validate the impression that the best goods and services are readily available.

In summer 2001, the Westchester was experiencing healthy levels of traffic and store sales were up compared to the year before. According to manager Robert Guerra, this was due to the most basic factor of all for a retail mall: a strong line-up of stores, and especially the high quality of the anchor establishments at the Westchester.

OPPOSITE: PREMIER FACILITIES SUCH AS THE CROWNE PLAZA HOTEL, THIS ONE IN DOWNTOWN WHITE PLAINS, CAN BE COUNTED ON FOR EVERY AMENITY— DOWN TO THEIR VERY OWN STATE-OF-THE-ART CONVENTION CENTERS.

Photo: Courtesy, Crowne Plaza White Plains/Regency Studios

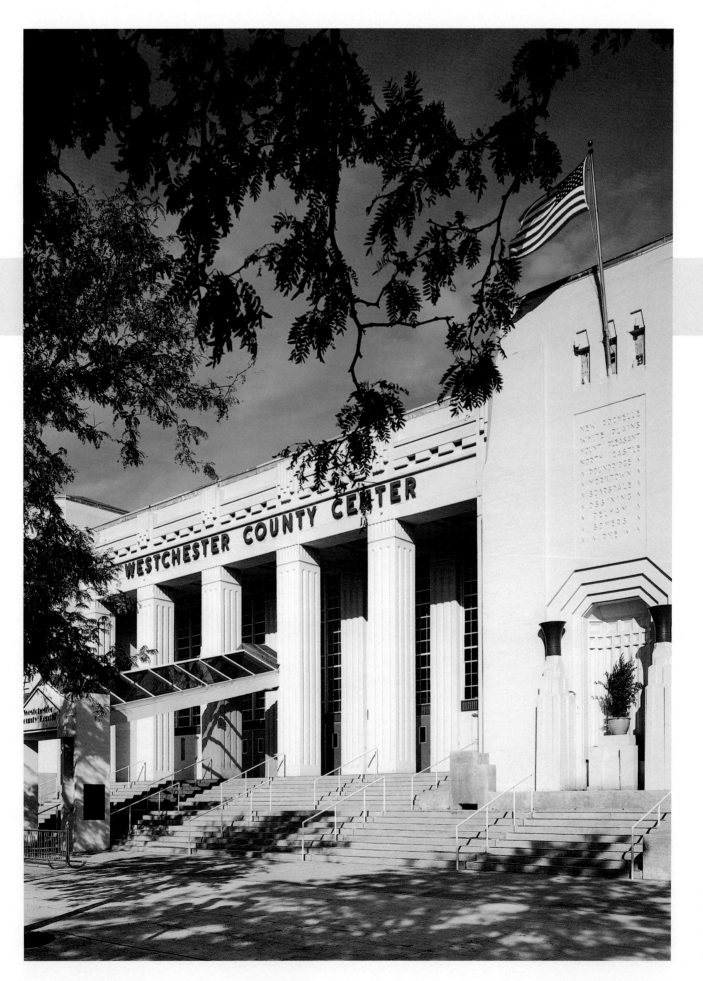

Photo: SuperStock, Inc.

The Westchester, however, is not the biggest in the county; that prize goes to the Cross County Shopping Center in Yonkers, with its 1,190,000 square feet featuring a multiplex movie house and 109 stores anchored by a Sears and a Stern's Department Store. This middle-class facility draws customers from all over the region, including New York City and the counties to the north.

In addition to its wide selection of retail stores, the county has almost 4,500 businesses that deal with entertainment, recreation, and the arts, including 116 performing arts companies.

One other thing that makes a place special is the quality of its restaurants, and Westchester County's is exceptional, providing for all tastes. In this one locale, there are almost 2,400 dining and beverage spots, ranging from the humble to the sublime. The county is even home to *The Wine Enthusiast* magazine (in Elmsford), to which people all over the country turn for the latest trends and advice.

ABOVE: THE BLOOMINGDALE'S PARKING LOT IS ALWAYS A GOOD INDICATOR OF THE COUNTY'S RETAIL HEALTH. BELOW: PRACTICE MAKES PERFECT FOR AN ACTOR WITH ONE OF THE AREA'S LEADING THEATER COMPANIES. OPPOSITE: AN ART DECO GEM, THIS CONVENTION CENTER IS A FAVORITE IN THE REGION. OVERLEAF: IT'S A NEW LEASE ON LIFE FOR A COUPLE ENJOYING THE GREAT OUTDOORS AT CROTON POINT.

THE CITY THAT ROCKS

Some venues in Westchester's cornucopia of entertainment opportunities are unique. New Roc City, for example, the crown jewel of New Rochelle's ongoing effort to develop its downtown, is a multimedia entertainment and retail complex opened in fall 1999. The scale is impressive, as are its statistics: New Roc City totals 1.2 million square feet, of which 500,000 are set aside for new retail establishments. A 124-suite Marriott Residence Inn (whose profits place it in the top 10 percent of all outlets in this chain) and 98 apartment units are part of the development.

Among the entertainment options in New Roc City is Regal Cinemas, a multiplex with 18 state-of-the-art theaters. The centerpiece of the development, however, is the Regal IMAX, the

Photos: Top, © Susan Oristaglio/Esto; bottom, © Digital Stock

9

Photo: Scott Barrow Inc./stock Barrow

its kind in the Northeast, which blasts riders 235 feet straight up into the air; laser tag, bumper cars, and a Kidz Zone; and Sports Plus, a 130,000-square-foot recreation facility that offers two skating rinks (including an NHL regulation-size hockey rink), virtual reality games, and a climbing wall. New Roc City also offers bowling alleys, a two-story Bally's Total Fitness Center, restaurants such as Applebee's Neighborhood Grill and Bar and the Rio Bravo Cantina, and even a Super Stop and Shop supermarket (the county's largest market).

All of this in a setting designed to maximize retail traffic downtown. The complex was deliberately planned so that each tenant would have its own street entrance, enabling customers to walk through the larger city as they peruse what New Roc City has to offer. This, in turn, encourages customers to explore the local setting. About four million people visit New Roc City each year, adding a huge shot of adrenaline to the local economy.

DISTINCTIVE DIVERSIONS

Rye Playland, a great example of local attractions, opened in 1928 when the

first and only facility of its kind in the county and one of the few in the region. Up to 320 patrons at a time can watch images on a screen that soars up six stories and listen to dialogue, music, and sound effects on a 12,000-watt, six-channel high-fidelity sound system. All of this adding up, of course, to a multilayered experience as the sheer scope of image and sound engulfs the audience. Because of the appeal of this kind of facility, as well as that of New Roc City itself, out of 263 theaters Regal maintains in New York and New Jersey, this IMAX is the eighth best performer—a rather astounding fact given that the large movie theaters in Manhattan are part of this pool.

Additional entertainment at the complex includes the Huguenot Tower Space Shot Ride, the only attraction of

ABOVE: YONKERS RACEWAY, HOME TO ONE LEG OF HARNESS RACING'S TRIPLE CROWN, IS ALSO A GOOD BET FOR FLEA MARKETS, COMMUNITY EVENTS, AND THE ANNUAL COUNTY FAIR. OPPOSITE: LITTLE ONES GET READY FOR A SPIN IN KIDDYLAND AT RYE'S HISTORIC ART DECO AMUSEMENT PARK, PLAYLAND, ON LONG ISLAND SOUND.

county decided to create a masterpiece for its elaborate parks system. Officials hired the influential firm of Walker and Gillette to design a series of art deco structures, which eventually paid off in unprecedented prestige: the only art deco amusement park in the United States, Rye Playland was named a National Historic Landmark.

The structures are gorgeous to look at, but Playland also delivers fun, with 45 major rides including roller coasters and a log flume. Five of the original rides, old-fashioned pleasures like the Whip, are still in operation, and in case people think the park is for old fogies, they

Photo: © SuperStock, Inc.

Photo: © Norman Owen Tomalin/Bruce Coleman, Inc.

ABOVE: MAMARONECK'S WINGED FOOT GOLF CLUB WILL HOST THE U.S. OPEN IN 2006. BELOW: THE SWIFT POCANTICO RIVER WAS A LATE-18TH-CENTURY FISHING SPOT OF LITERARY GREAT WASHINGTON IRVING. OPPOSITE: SLEEPY HOLLOW CEMETERY, IRVING'S RESTING PLACE, DATES TO THE LATE 1600s.

The county is crowded with historic sites to visit, places like Washington's Headquarters Museum in North White Plains, the White Plains National Battlefield Site, and the Bedford Historical Society's Federal Style Courthouse/Museum. This last structure, a lovely example of Dutch and federal architecture, was built in 1787, making it the oldest county government building.

The resting place of Washington Irving in Sleepy Hollow Cemetery is a local landmark. Visitors often stop off in thanks for his wonderful tale that, with new versions still appearing, seems likely to entrance readers forever. While there, some bow their head—in part homage to the author, in part recognition that they, unlike one of his lead characters, still have one.

Washington Irving's wonderful imagination still speaks to us. Close to two centuries ago, Irving recognized Westchester County as one of the nation's garden spots. Succeeding generations have built on this paradise, turning it into a magnificent place to do business or enjoy life's pleasures. As Irving noted, it is a charming, radiant place to live and work, where only one's ability to dream limits what can be accomplished.

should try the recently opened Double Shot, which launches 12 riders straight up into the air at 40 miles an hour; they reach the top of the 85-foot tower in under two seconds. The day after the ride opened, a student who had just earned her diploma gravely commented that graduating high school was nothing compared to riding the Double Shot: "This takes guts." A lot of people must have that particular attribute, since Playland gets 1.1 million visitors a year.

Westchester County also has an extensive network of parks and nature preserves, lush sites for hiking, swimming, and picnics. There are seven public and 42 private golf courses, some of which are part of the nation's finest country clubs. The sport of kings, horse racing, takes place at Yonkers Raceway, and those who like to compete themselves run in the yearly Yonkers Marathon and Half Marathon—one of the oldest events of its kind in America, the first race having been run in 1918.

Photos: Top, Susan Oristaglio/Esto; bottom, courtesy, Rockefeller State Park Preserve

Photo: © Lee Snider/CORBIS

9

Part Two

Partners in

Progress
PROFILES OF CORPORATIONS & ORGANIZATIONS

Photo: © CORBIS Stock Market/Mug Shots

Profiles

Education

Photo: © CORBIS

PACE UNIVERSITY

*The motto for Pace University is **Opportunitas**. For nearly a century, the university, with its extraordinary track record of rigorous higher education, progressive community service, and farsighted business and corporate liaison, has made that motto live with relevance, accomplishment, and vision.*

Partnering for Opportunity: Pace University & Westchester County

In 1963, when Pace opened its Pleasantville Campus in Westchester County, it initiated a partnership rich in opportunities for both partners—the county as well as the university. Pace could find no better location than Westchester County for extending its institutional mission. The area, one of the nation's most renowned "suburbs," actually offers a vast menu of opportunities for working, living, learning, and playing. It is a county of cities as well as country roads and towns. It is the location of industrial parks, corporate headquarters, and Revolutionary War landmarks. It offers a world-class medical center and stunning vistas of the Hudson River. It is home to traditional winding-lane communities and serene forested parks. It is a progressive business, educational, cultural, and social environment. It is quite a place.

A HISTORY OF GROWTH

Pace University is quite an institution. Founded in lower Manhattan in 1906 by Charles and Homer Pace as an accounting and business law school, Pace Institute, as it was called, became a degree-granting college as early as 1948 and a full-fledged university in 1973, offering graduate and undergraduate degrees and professional degrees in nursing and law. Pace University grew rapidly at both its Manhattan and Westchester campuses. The Undergraduate School of Business Administration, the School of Arts and Sciences, and the School of Education

ABOVE: CHOATE HOUSE, LOCATED ON THE PLEASANTVILLE CAMPUS, IS HOST TO MANY ACTIVITIES, AND IS THE SITE OF THE PACE UNIVERSITY ART GALLERY. BELOW: THE BRIARCLIFF CAMPUS'S DOW HALL PROVIDES A VARIETY OF COMFORTABLE LIVING ARRANGEMENTS FOR BOTH MEN AND WOMEN.

were established in 1965. In 1966, the Leinhard School of Nursing opened on the Pleasantville campus. In the 1970s, Pace absorbed the College of White Plains and acquired the assets of Briarcliff College. The Briarcliff site became home for an IBM international education center, the Hastings Center, and a NYNEX Center. The School of Computer Science and Information Systems was established in 1983. By the turn of the century, Pace had collaborated with Marist College and the State University of New York at New Paltz to create the Hudson Valley Center for Emerging Technologies (HVCET); had broken ground for the Ann and Alfred Goldstein Health, Fitness, and Recreation Center at the Pleasantville campus; and had begun work on the Judicial Institute of the State of New York. Enrollment has risen to 14,000 students, with all U.S. states and dozens of foreign countries represented.

Pace University has become an integral part of Westchester County, contributing in countless ways to the revitalization of its cities, the growth and well being of its population, the health and vitality of its business community, and the diversification of its culture. Westchester County, in turn, has become a supportive and resourceful

A FUTURE OF SERVICE

The history of Pace is not defined by its growth and development, but by the many services it renders to the members of its academic community and to the greater community of Westchester County. A very few of these are:

HVCET—The goals of this unique collaboration among Hudson Valley institutions of higher learning, including Pace, are to provide a research base in emerging technologies to support existing businesses as they venture into e-business and to attract new business to the region.

CENTER FOR COMMUNITY OUTREACH—This program is designed to get Pace students involved in community service during and after their academic careers.

ABOVE: THE EDWARD AND DORIS MORTOLA LIBRARY IS LOCATED ON PACE UNIVERSITY'S PLEASANTVILLE CAMPUS.

THE NEW YORK JUDICIAL INSTITUTE—Located at the Pace University School of Law on the White Plains campus, this is the first training and research facility in the nation built by and for a state court system. Besides providing a forum for identifying new trends affecting the judicial system, it offers the judicial and lay community at large opportunities for continuing education courses, seminars, and conferences.

COMPUTER LITERACY OPPORTUNITY OUTREACH TRAINING—In partnership with the Westchester County Department of Social Service, Pace provides public assistance recipients with employment-directed education.

PACE HISPANIC OUTREACH PROGRAM (PHOP)—Initiated a dozen years ago in partnership with the White Plains City School District and Centro Hispanico, a community-based organization, PHOP is a mentoring program that utilizes the volunteer services of Pace students to guide and inspire Hispanic elementary, middle school, and high school students to seriously consider preparing for a college education. Formal evaluation of the program indicates that 100 percent of PHOP participants plan to attend college.

THE PACE COMPUTER LEARNING CENTER—Founded in 1984 by Pace University's School of Computer Science and Information Systems, the Pace Computer Learning Center has provided more than 30,000 days of corporate training. Customized, hands-on instruction, available at a variety of locations, helps meet the needs of the business community.

partner in the rapid growth and development of Pace University. It is, indeed, a working partnership and a partnership that works.

LEFT: DAVID A. CAPUTO IS PRESIDENT OF PACE UNIVERSITY. RIGHT, INSET: THE EVELYN AND JOSEPH I. LUBIN GRADUATE CENTER IS LOCATED ON THE WHITE PLAINS CAMPUS. RIGHT: THE ANN AND ALFRED GOLDSTEIN HEALTH, FITNESS, AND RECREATION CENTER, LOCATED ON THE PLEASANTVILLE CAMPUS, IS SCHEDULED FOR COMPLETION IN FALL 2002.

THE COLLEGE OF NEW ROCHELLE

At The College of New Rochelle are the School of Arts and Sciences for women and coeducational schools including the School of Nursing, the School of New Resources, and the Graduate School.

If humankind's need for creative and responsible use of reason seized the world's heart with inconceivable force on September 11, 2001, that need has long motivated compassionate educators. Among them was the Order of St. Ursula's Mother Irene Gill, who founded The College of New Rochelle in 1904 with 12 undergraduates.

New York State's first Catholic college for women, and one of just 62 women's colleges in the United States, The College of New Rochelle (CNR) today imaginatively integrates collegiate traditions of proven worth with contemporary strategies to bring quality education to diverse and crucial groups of adult and traditional-age learners. With a student-to-faculty ratio of 10 to one, the college's four schools and seven campuses serve more than 7,000 students. CNR's extended family of some 31,000 graduates includes company presidents, judges, nurses and doctors, journalists, artists, teachers, scientists, and many who have devoted their lives to family, public, and religious service.

On the college's main campus in suburban Westchester County—20 beautiful acres 16 miles north of Manhattan—20 major buildings surround historic Leland Castle, the college's first home. At the intellectual center rises the Mother Irene Gill Memorial Library, where a multimillion-dollar renovation completed in January 2002 showcases a superb research collection of more than 200,000 volumes and up-to-the-minute educational technology tools. From spacious private study rooms to abundant computer workstations, this dynamic environment beckons students and scholars to achieve their intellects' highest promise. Adjacent are four residence halls, two modern science buildings, a majestic chapel, and—something of a collegiate crown jewel—the Mooney Center.

With its H. W. Taylor Institute for Entrepreneurial Studies, ultramodern Romita Auditorium, television studio, model classroom, and art, communications, and computer facilities, the Mooney Center allows students, faculty and staff, alumnae/i, and people from business and other professional enterprises to interact in an invigorating dynamic of lifelong learning.

THE COMMITMENT TO WOMEN'S EDUCATION IS A HALLMARK AT THE COLLEGE OF NEW ROCHELLE, AS EVIDENCED BY THE COLLEGE'S NEARLY CENTURY-LONG TRADITION OF EDUCATING WOMEN TO TAKE ON LEADERSHIP ROLES IN THEIR CAREERS AND THEIR COMMUNITIES.

THE SCHOOLS OF CNR

Although The College of New Rochelle's three other schools are fully coeducational, the **School of Arts and Sciences**, on CNR's main campus, continues to enroll only women. Its undergraduate program includes all of the traditional disciplines of the liberal arts and science as well as a number of professionally oriented fields. While mastering a rigorous liberal arts curriculum in an environment embracing diversity and an expanding sense of community, young women here can acquire the solid foundation of skills and values upon which to build rich and productive lifetimes.

LEFT: FROM ART AND COMMUNICATIONS TO EDUCATION, NURSING, AND SOCIAL WORK, THE COLLEGE OF NEW ROCHELLE OFFERS A DIVERSE RANGE OF UNDERGRADUATE AND GRADUATE DEGREE PROGRAMS IN A DYNAMIC LEARNING ENVIRONMENT. BELOW: STUDENTS MAY TAKE ADVANTAGE OF THE STATE-OF-THE-ART EDUCATIONAL AND TECHNOLOGICAL TOOLS AVAILABLE IN THE NEWLY RENOVATED GILL LIBRARY.

Responding to the needs of working professionals seeking advanced degrees, the **Graduate School**, inaugurated in 1969, provides courses in the evenings, on weekends, and in summer. Programs in art, communication studies, education, and human services emphasize the theoretical foundations, research data, methods, and materials of these professional disciplines as well as practical knowledge and field-based education.

Respected nationwide, the **School of Nursing**, established in 1976, offers undergraduate and graduate programs that provide the solid professional foundation upon which nearly limitless specialization may be built—including emergency care, surgical nursing, and newborn intensive care. Included are the four-year bachelor of science in nursing (B.S.N.), an accelerated program for Registered Nurses seeking the B.S.N., and several master's tracks.

Perhaps the most dramatic evidence of CNR's far-sighted commitment to the multiple communities it serves lies in its **School of New Resources**, founded in 1972. The school's baccalaureate liberal arts program is designed for adults over 21 years old and integrates life experience into the curriculum. With seven branch campuses in New Rochelle and throughout New York City, for 30 years the school

has brought the educational experience directly into the community where adults live and work. Innovative local campuses—in Brooklyn, Co-op City, the South Bronx, New Rochelle, Harlem, and in Manhattan on West 29th Street and at District Council 37 Union Headquarters on East 2nd Street—provide user-friendly integrated technologies, computer-assisted classrooms and laboratories, technology-based learning, multipurpose resource centers, and on-line reference libraries.

In describing what The College of New Rochelle seeks to accomplish on all her campuses, president Stephen J. Sweeny says, "We at CNR model for society an environment that values diversity, promotes tolerance for difference, and prizes justice. This is achieved by fulfilling our mission as a university: to provide safe space—sacred space—where people can discover and strengthen their dignity and, with this reinforced self worth, can move out to change the world."

MERCY COLLEGE

With five campuses in Westchester County and New York City, plus Extension Centers and a distance learning program, Mercy College offers associate, undergraduate, and graduate degrees to students worldwide.

MERCY COLLEGE'S 60-ACRE DOBBS FERRY CAMPUS OVERLOOKS THE MYSTIC HUDSON RIVER.

body, and the college has emerged as a national model of success for students who are motivated to pursue a degree but are unable to attend a traditional education institution.

Mercy attracts students from more than 100 countries, and 70 percent of its students will be the first in their family to earn a college degree. Approximately 7,000 students, with an average age of 28, are pursuing under-graduate degrees with a strong liberal arts foundation. More than 700 full- and part-time students are pursuing associate degrees. Mercy's 2,700 graduate students, average age 36, are working toward degrees primarily in the fields of health, education, and business.

Students say that the things that distinguish an education at Mercy College are quality degree programs, flexible scheduling, low tuition, and a personalized education in a caring environment.

Today, Mercy College is one of the largest independent, coeducational four-year colleges in New York State. The college's main campus is in Dobbs Ferry, in Westchester County, with branch campuses in Yorktown Heights, White Plains, the Bronx, and Manhattan. Mercy College also maintains Extension Centers in Westchester County and New York City, as well as offering a variety of distance learning courses.

Despite Mercy's expansive academic network, each campus is designed to provide a personal atmosphere. Academic Advisors work with students to help shape the content and direction of their college careers. In addition, classes are small, with an average student-to-faculty ratio of 17 to one.

FLEXIBLE CLASS SCHEDULES

Mercy College is committed to serving the community by providing education for students on either traditional or nontraditional schedules. The current enrollment of almost 10,000 represents a diverse student

A BROAD RANGE OF ACADEMIC PROGRAMS

Although the liberal arts are a key focus, Mercy's more than 90 graduate, undergraduate, and pre-professional programs embrace a range of disciplines, including Business, Education, Communications, Health Sciences, and Liberal Arts. Recognized as a rapidly growing center for graduate education, Mercy offers more than 26 master's programs, from Psychology and English Literature to Banking and Physical Therapy.

Both graduate and undergraduate courses are available through flexible scheduling of day, evening, weekend, and on-line classes.

Mercy College's Distance Learning program, MerLIN, provides a way to obtain a quality college education via the Internet. MerLIN, introduced in 1990, now has over 150 courses available on-line. B.A. and M.S. degrees can be earned by students not only in New York, but across the nation and around the world.

Both photos: © CORBIS

Profiles

Financial

Services

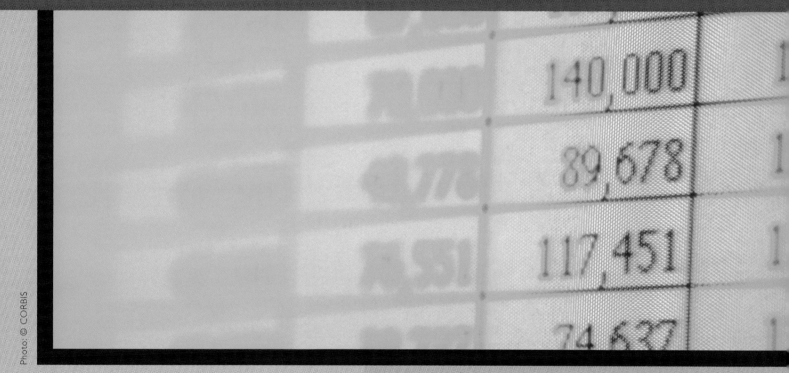

Photo: © CORBIS

THE BANK OF NEW YORK

The Bank of New York today provides a full spectrum of global financial services for businesses and individuals.

THE NATION'S OLDEST BANK AND ONE OF THE LARGEST FINANCIAL HOLDING COMPANIES IN THE UNITED STATES, THE BANK OF NEW YORK, HEADQUARTERED AT ONE WALL STREET IN NEW YORK CITY, PROVIDES A COMPLETE RANGE OF BANKING AND OTHER FINANCIAL SERVICES TO CORPORATIONS AND INDIVIDUALS ACROSS THE GREATER NEW YORK METROPOLITAN AREA AND THROUGH SUBSIDIARIES IN THE UNITED STATES AND WORLDWIDE.

with assets of $89.3 billion, and total shareholders' equity exceeding $6.5 billion. It has branches in foreign locations, representative offices in 15 others, and subsidiaries and affiliates in every major international location—amounting to an international network of more than 2,300 correspondent banks worldwide. In the United States, The Bank of New York has approximately 345 branches in the New York metropolitan area, plus subsidiaries on both coasts and throughout the South, the North, and the Midwest.

A HISTORY OF SOUND FINANCIAL POLICIES

"Throughout its history, The Bank of New York has been vitally important in building America's economic leadership," says John Tolomer, senior vice president of the Westchester/Rockland/Connecticut Regional Commercial Banking Division. "During the course of its business life, the bank has prevailed through six major financial panics and 10 economic depressions and has seen the nation shaken by seven wars. In spite of such crises, however, with the exception of a one-year moratorium imposed by the government, The Bank of New York has paid dividends every year throughout its more than 200-year history. This is in large part because, in spite of the speculative temptations offered by a burgeoning economy, the Bank has stayed true to

The Bank of New York is not only the oldest bank in the nation, it also is one of the oldest banks in the world. Established in 1784 by Alexander Hamilton before he became Secretary of the Treasury in George Washington's cabinet, it was the first bank ever to extend credit to the United States government. The loan amount was for $200,000, and by extending the loan, The Bank of New York helped to establish the economic independence of the young nation.

Today, The Bank of New York is one of the largest financial holding companies in the United States, the sound fiscal policies laid down by its founders."

At the launch of the New York Stock Exchange in 1792, the first corporate stock to be traded was The Bank of New York. In that same year, The Bank of New York loaned money for the construction of factories in New Jersey, marking the beginning of the Bank's role in the economic growth of New York's metropolitan area. Since then The Bank of New York has had a major involvement in financing the construction of New York's transport systems, including its waterways, railroads, and the New York City subways.

SHOWN ABOVE IS THE 1972 SCARSDALE SITE OF A BRANCH OF THE FORMER IRVING TRUST COMPANY, WHICH WAS ACQUIRED IN 1988 BY THE BANK OF NEW YORK, CREATING THE NATION'S 10TH LARGEST BANK AT THAT TIME AND SETTING THE STAGE FOR THE BANK'S FULL-SERVICE FINANCIAL INSTITUTION OF TODAY.

EXPANDING BUSINESS OFFERINGS AND A NETWORK OF BRANCH BANKS

In 1922 soon after the United States became the largest creditor nation as well as the world's new international money center, The Bank of New York merged with the New York Life Insurance and Trust Company, adding an important trust business to its operations.

In 1948 The Bank of New York merged with Fifth Avenue Bank, and in 1966 the Empire Trust Company. The Bank began extending its financial services to businesses and individuals throughout New York City, and then beyond the city's borders, establishing one of the largest networks of suburban branch banks in the United States. Next, it extended service to major corporations across the nation and to special industries.

Global expansion began with an office in London in 1966. But a major breakthrough occurred with the acquisition of The Irving Bank corporation in 1988. This transaction, between two highly complementary institutions, created the 10th largest bank in the nation at that time and set the stage for The Bank of New York today.

FULL-SPECTRUM, STATE-OF-THE-ART SERVICES

Today, The Bank of New York provides full-spectrum, state-of-the art banking and other financial services to corporations and individuals worldwide. It offers corporate banking, international banking, investor and issuer securities services, asset management, and global payment services.

The Bank is widely acknowledged as one of the largest providers of global securities services, offering the widest range of capabilities available. In fact, it is ranked number one or number two in the majority of the markets it serves.

Additionally, in funds transfer, The Bank of New York is the only bank to have significantly increased its market share since 1995.

Tolomer concluded, "The Bank of New York today is ready to meet the challenges and opportunities of a rapidly changing global financial services marketplace."

HSBC Bank USA

HSBC Bank USA, based in Buffalo, provides its customers with more than 415 branch banks statewide,

offering business and personal financial services with a firm commitment to ever greater customer satisfaction.

"One team, one priority: satisfied customers." This has been the motto of Buffalo-based HSBC Bank USA throughout its more than 150-year history.

In keeping with this motto, HSBC is focused on being the best when it comes to providing commercial, corporate, institutional, and retail customers with financial services. And with assets, combined with those of its U.S. holding company, New York City–based HSBC USA, Inc., of more than $85 billion, it is well positioned to provide the best.

Moreover, with 415 branch banks statewide, including 27 in Westchester County, plus eight branches in Florida, two in Pennsylvania, three in California, and 17 in Panama, HSBC has the facilities to make it easy for customers to avail themselves of its services. In fact, it has the most extensive branch network of any bank operating in the Empire State.

What distinguishes HSBC, however, is its commitment to its customers with full understanding of their needs and consistent delivery on its promises. To achieve these goals, the bank's employees work as a team, looking at every one of their actions from their customers' perspectives, striving to give customers even more satisfaction today than yesterday.

Further distinguishing HSBC is its association with London-based HSBC Holdings plc, one of the largest and oldest financial services organizations in the world. Its companies comprise HSBC Group, of which HSBC Bank USA is an indirectly held, wholly owned subsidiary. As part of the HSBC Group network of 6,500 offices in 78 countries and territories in Europe, the Asia-Pacific region, the Americas, the Middle East, and Africa, HSBC Bank USA can offer its customers a global reach and a range of financial services unparalleled in the banking industry. For example, HSBC customers can access any one of the more than 600,000 ATMs the HSBC Group maintains in more than 100 countries.

But the HSBC Bank thrust doesn't end with financial services. It has a strong commitment to community service. The bank strives to focus 75 percent of its

THE HEADQUARTERS BUILDING FOR HSBC BANK USA IS LOCATED IN DUFFALO, NEW YORK. THE BANK ALSO OFFERS 415 BRANCH BANKS STATEWIDE, INCLUDING 27 IN WESTCHESTER COUNTY.

philanthropic giving primarily in two critical areas—education and the environment. In addition, it contributes monetarily and provides in-kind services to a variety of charitable causes.

Furthermore, the bank is focused on revitalizing neighborhoods within the communities it serves and helping people in need. It has programs for providing low-cost loans to home buyers with low-to-moderate incomes, and it provides grants and reduced-interest financing to assist in the redevelopment of neighborhoods.

GROWING STRONG ROOTS

HSBC Bank's roots in the United States date back to 1850 when its predecessor, the Marine Trust Company in Buffalo, was established to finance shipping trade on the Great Lakes. For 130 years the bank thrived and grew, eventually becoming Marine Midland Bank. In 1980, the HSBC Group acquired 51 percent of the bank, which became a wholly owned subsidiary in 1987.

In 1999, the name Marine Midland Bank was changed to HSBC Bank USA as the bank joined the HSBC Group's worldwide rebranding effort to strengthen recognition of the group as one of the world's most customer-oriented financial services organizations. Also in 1999, HSBC acquired Republic National Bank of New York, further strengthening HSBC Bank USA's position in the New York financial market.

BUILDING ON A SOLID FOUNDATION

HSBC Bank USA has continually built on its predecessors' banking innovations and commitment to customer service. As a result, it offers customers all of the products available within the banking industry today, and then some.

For retail customers, it offers a variety of checking and savings accounts, insurance, investing opportunities, credit cards, and mortgages and home equity and

ABOVE: SHOWN HERE IS THE HSBC USA HEADQUARTERS, ON 5TH AVENUE IN NEW YORK CITY. BELOW LEFT: THIS HSBC BRANCH IS IN SCARSDALE, NEW YORK.

student loans. On-line banking is available and growing by leaps and bounds each day.

For business customers, the bank offers, in addition to the fundamental business banking products, a host of services such as programs for raising investment capital, setting up corporate trusts, making and receiving payments, managing retirement funds, and making international and domestic investments.

In short, like Westchester County, HSBC Bank USA offers all of its constituents an infinite array of "golden opportunities."

Profiles

Health Care &

Pharmaceuticals

Photo: © CORBIS

SOUND SHORE HEALTH SYSTEM, INC.

Sound Shore Health System, Inc., is a fully integrated regional health care delivery system offering emergency, primary, specialty, and long-term care, and ancillary services.

One of the largest not-for-profit private health care systems between New York City and Albany, Sound Shore Health System, Inc. (SSHS) consists of Sound Shore Medical Center of Westchester, The Mount Vernon Hospital, The Dorothea Hopfer School of Nursing, The Sound Shore Extended Care and Rehabilitation Center, and Visiting Nurse Association of Hudson Valley. With these components, Sound Shore provides a comprehensive array of high quality, compassionate, patient-centered programs in emergency, primary, specialty, and long-term care, along with a full range of ancillary services. A regional teaching institution and major affiliate of New York Medical College, SSHS is committed to providing excellence in patient care, as well as a supportive environment for graduate medical education and clinical research. SSHS offers highly respected residency programs in Medicine, Surgery, Anesthesiology, Pediatrics, and Pathology with Fellowship Programs in Laparoscopic Surgery, Endocrinology, and Gastroenterology.

THE SOUND SHORE MEDICAL CENTER OF WESTCHESTER AMBULATORY SURGERY CENTER AT THE SUREN AND VIRGINIA FESJIAN PAVILION PROVIDES DISTINGUISHED LAPAROSCOPIC, ORTHOPAEDIC, SPINE, AND GENERAL SURGERY.

A REGIONAL HEALTH CARE LEADER

Meeting the challenges of an ever-changing health care environment, Sound Shore Health System, with more than 700 affiliated physicians, is an established leader in the health care industry. In recognition of the quality and scope of care provided, the New York State Department of Health has designated Sound Shore Health System as the area's Regional Trauma Center and approved the establishment of the Naomi and Isaac Kaplan Level II Nursery and the Harriet and Bernard Miller Adult Cardiac Catheterization Laboratory on its campus. Other regional centers of excellence include the Klein Antepartum Testing Laboratory; the Solomon Katz Breast Center; The Goldstein Cancer Center; the Ludington Adult Day Services Center; Joslin Diabetes Center; Orthopaedic, Neurological, and Spine Surgery Center; the Geriatric Institute; Family Health and Wellness Center; Mental Health Service; Chronic Wound Treatment and Hyperbaric Center; Acupuncture and Oriental Medicine Program; Sleep Diagnostic Center; and the Gastric-Reflux Center.

FORGING DYNAMIC PARTNERSHIPS

"Sound Shore Health System has maximized the opportunities of a challenging health care environment in order to better serve our communities," says John R. Spicer, president. "We have developed new clinical initiatives; expanded services; recruited outstanding physicians, nurses and health care professionals, and forged dynamic partnerships with academic and other health care institutions. We have created opportunities for trustees, volunteers, friends, donors, and patients to form partnerships with us in fulfilling our mission. Our commitment is first and foremost to our patients and their families, and it is our intention to provide the highest quality, most comprehensive spectrum of accessible, affordable, and compassionate care."

In recent years, Spicer and Sound Shore Health System were founding members of Pinnacle Healthcare, Inc., a partnership that includes—in addition to SSHS— Westchester Medical Center, Riverside Health Care

System, and Hudson Valley Hospital Center. This innovative health care affiliation ensures that residents of Westchester may address virtually all health care concerns without ever having to leave the county.

CARE IN THE 21ST CENTURY

With a rich legacy of more than a century of service to Westchester County, Sound Shore Health System is well positioned to provide leadership and care in the new millennium. Evidence of that capability may be found in the Katz Breast Center, where state-of-the-art screening, diagnostic resources, and skilled clinicians provide care to women, including those with breast disease. Using a multidisciplinary team approach, the center prepares expert education and treatment plans combining the expertise of leading medical and radiation oncologists, breast surgeons, breast imaging radiologists, and pathologists. Completing this team are nurses, technicians, and social workers who help to meet the medical, emotional, and psychological needs of both patients and families.

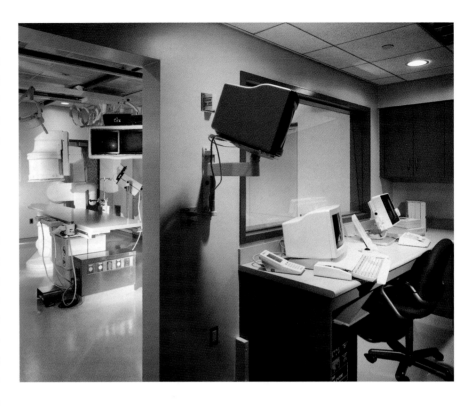

ABOVE: AT THE HARRIET AND BERNARD MILLER ADULT CARDIAC CATHETERIZATION LABORATORY, SPECIALIZED CARDIAC TEAMS PROVIDE ADVANCED DIAGNOSTIC PROCEDURES. BELOW: STEPHEN PIAZZA, M.D., IS THE DIRECTOR OF THE NAOMI AND ISAAC KAPLAN LEVEL II NURSERY. © JOE VERICKER/**PHOTOBUREAU**, INC.

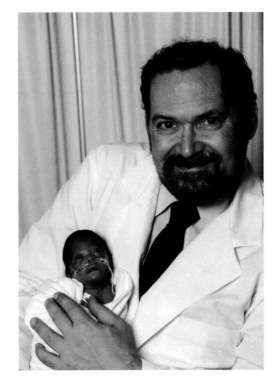

In Westchester County, Sound Shore Health System provides high quality care for people of all ages. Young families have access to unique programs for high-risk pregnancies and medically fragile newborns. Cardiac patients requiring accomplished clinicians and leading-edge technology may take advantage of the Miller Adult Cardiac Catheterization Laboratory, where specialized cardiac teams provide advanced diagnostic procedures in comfortable, modern surroundings. Older adults may access social and medical adult day services, rehabilitation programs, and nursing home care. Patients requiring surgery receive superior care from distinguished laparoscopic, orthopaedic, spine, and general surgeons in the comfort and distinctive surroundings of the Suren and Virginia Fesjian Pavilion.

The Sound Shore Health System is a leading health care resource for southern Westchester, providing advanced and compassionate care for the county's diverse range of health care needs. It is a system that truly provides "Care. For Life."

BAYER DIAGNOSTICS

A leader in its field, Bayer Diagnostics designs, manufactures, and markets innovative medical diagnostics systems that touch the lives of five million patients in 100 countries every day.

When it comes to meeting the medical diagnostics needs of health care providers and patients around the world, Tarrytown, New York–based Bayer Diagnostics is one of the most recognized diagnostics businesses, with annual sales close to $2 billion.

Bayer Diagnostics develops, manufactures, and markets technologies used in the assessment and management of health, including the areas of cardiovascular and kidney disease, oncology, virology, and diabetes. Its army of products and technologies assists physicians, medical laboratories, hospitals, clinics, and patients in early diagnosis, effective disease management, and monitoring of such maladies as heart disease, cancer, anemia, diabetes, hepatitis, HIV, and various congenital diseases.

A member of the Bayer Group, one of the largest international health care and chemical companies in the world—Bayer Diagnostics employs more than 7,000 individuals committed to making a positive difference to human health. Distinguished by its commitment to quality, Bayer Diagnostics is dedicated to surpassing customer expectations, from providing state-of-the-art products to offering unparalleled service and support.

TODAY, THE PIONEERING SPIRIT OF BAYER DIAGNOSTICS IS STRONGER THAN EVER, AS IS THE COMPANY'S COMMITMENT TO DEVELOP PRODUCTS AND PROCESSES THAT DETECT, MONITOR, AND MANAGE DISEASE EVER MORE EFFECTIVELY.

BENEFITS FOR PATIENTS WORLDWIDE

The state-of-the-art products of Bayer Diagnostics, sold in more than 100 countries, touch the lives of five million patients every day. Based in part on data provided by the products of Bayer Diagnostics, a treating physician may give a patient a clean bill of health or learn about a serious health challenge, work to stabilize a chronic condition, or prescribe the use of therapeutic treatment.

Besides its diagnostic products and services and its daily commitment to improving the quality of patients lives, Bayer Diagnostics is dedicated to building quality partnerships. With its operations organized geographically and aligned according to business segments, Bayer Diagnostics enables customers worldwide to benefit from its informed local leadership. Five major Bayer Diagnostics manufacturing plants, 50 branch offices, and an extensive network of distribution centers position the organization to meet customer needs in all key areas of the industry.

Approximately 800 Bayer Diagnostics employees are based in Tarrytown, which is home to the company's headquarters, as well as its Laboratory Testing business segment and U.S. commercial operations. Its other business segments—Self-Testing, Near Patient (point-of-care and critical care) Testing, and Nucleic Acid Diagnostics—are based, respectively, in Elkhart, Indiana; Medfield, Massachusetts; and Emeryville, California.

RIGHT: HEADQUARTERED IN TARRYTOWN, NEW YORK, BAYER DIAGNOSTICS HAS BEEN BRINGING IMPORTANT TECHNOLOGICAL DIAGNOSTICS ADVANCES TO HEALTH CARE CUSTOMERS FOR MORE THAN HALF A CENTURY. BELOW: THE COMPANY PROVIDES CUSTOMERS AROUND THE WORLD WITH WELL-KNOWN BRAND NAME PRODUCTS, SUCH AS GLUCOMETER® AND MULTISTIX®.

INNOVATIVE TESTING

Bayer Diagnostics has been bringing important technological diagnostics advances to health care customers for more than half a century. Backed by the vast resources of the Bayer Group and driven by a dedication to help physicians detect, monitor, and manage disease ever more effectively, Bayer Diagnostics has compiled a lengthy history of technological firsts, from setting new standards in diabetes management and introducing the world's first automated instrument for clinical chemistry, to bringing new molecular diagnostics technology to the health care market.

Today, Bayer remains committed to research and development programs that will maintain the organization's position at the very cutting edge of its industry.

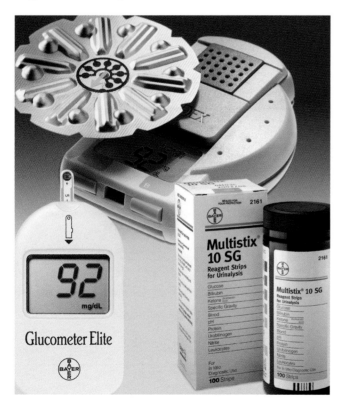

A POSITIVE DIFFERENCE FOR HUMAN HEALTH

Much of the growth of Bayer Diagnostics has come about as a result of strategic mergers with other leading medical diagnostics firms. Miles Inc. became a member of the Bayer family in 1978. Technicon Instruments, which introduced, among other things, the first fully automated blood chemistry analyzer to the health care marketplace, joined Bayer in 1989. And Chiron Diagnostics, a leader in the development of molecular diagnostics innovations for the quick and accurate detection of infectious diseases, became part of Bayer Diagnostics in 1998.

Along with its strategies for growth, Bayer Diagnostics pursues its mission of making a positive difference to human health. Today, the Bayer Diagnostics spirit and commitment to developing products and processes to detect, monitor, and manage disease ever more effectively is stronger than ever. This is good news for health care providers and patients in Westchester County and around the world.

WESTCHESTER MEDICAL CENTER

Serving the region with four major facilities, Westchester Medical Center's six Centers of Excellence are at the forefront of medical research and the latest advances in clinical health care.

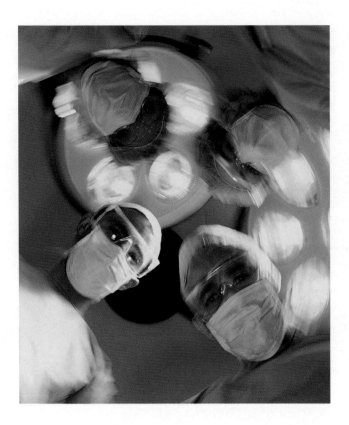

As an academic medical center and the region's advanced care and Level 1 Trauma Center, Westchester Medical Center (WMC) is on the leading edge of medical research and the latest advances in clinical care. WMC serves more than 3.6 million people in the seven-county New York Hudson Valley region, northern New Jersey, and lower Connecticut. Located on a beautiful 92-acre suburban campus in Valhalla, WMC's Centers of Excellence include the Transplant Center, Children's Hospital, the George E. Reed Heart Center, the Trauma and Burn Center, the Zalmen A. Arlin Cancer Institute, and the Neuroscience Center, as well as other programs.

With more than 1,000 beds in four major facilities—University Hospital, the Behavioral Health Center, the Taylor Care Center (for skilled nursing and subacute care), and the Westchester Institute for Human Development (for the developmentally disabled)—WMC's renowned specialty services have made it a referral hospital of choice for physicians and patients seeking the highest level and quality of care.

WINNER OF THE NATIONAL CONSUMER CHOICE AWARD FOR BEST HEART SERVICES, WESTCHESTER MEDICAL CENTER'S GEORGE E. REED HEART CENTER OFFERS THE REGION'S MOST COMPREHENSIVE RANGE OF ADVANCED HEART SERVICES, FROM TREATMENT OF PRENATAL HEART DEFECTS TO ADULT HEART TRANSPLANTS.

CENTERS OF EXCELLENCE

An academic affiliate of New York Medical College, Westchester Medical Center is home to the region's only Transplant Center and the state's largest kidney transplant program, as well as one of only four liver transplant programs and one of only six heart transplant programs in the state.

The Children's Hospital at WMC is the only all-specialty children's hospital in the region. Its renowned pediatric specialists—including pediatric neurosurgeons, pediatric open-heart surgeons, pediatric cardiologists, pediatric oncologists, and pediatric infectious disease specialists—treat more than 20,000 infants and children each year. The Children's Hospital provides the only Level IV regional neonatal intensive care unit, the region's only pediatric trauma center and pediatric intensive care unit, and a specialized high-risk obstetrics center.

All of WMC's highly regarded heart services are organized within the George E. Reed Heart Center, which ranks among the top 10 in the state for its cardiac surgery and cardiac catheterization programs. The center provides advanced cardiac medical diagnosis, treatment, and surgery to infants, children, and adults from the region and beyond for nearly every conceivable heart disorder. With its heart transplant program, established in 2001, WMC now offers all cardiovascular services.

WMC boasts the state's only trauma and burn center to have received the prestigious American College of Surgeons Verification. As a Level 1 Trauma Center, WMC is equipped to handle the region's most critical trauma cases. Each year, approximately 13,000 adults and children come through the doors of its Trauma Center/Emergency Department.

LEFT: TWO MEDEVAC HELICOPTERS AND SPECIALLY TRAINED STAT FLIGHT TEAMS RESPOND TO EMERGENCIES OVER A 5,000-SQUARE-MILE AREA TO DELIVER PATIENTS TO MEDICAL FACILITIES, PROVIDING ADVANCED MEDICAL CARE DURING TRANSIT. WESTCHESTER MEDICAL CENTER HAS THE STATE'S ONLY TRAUMA AND BURN CENTER TO HAVE RECEIVED THE PRESTIGIOUS AMERICAN COLLEGE OF SURGEON'S VERIFICATION. BELOW: AS THE REGION'S ONLY ADVANCED CARE UNIVERSITY MEDICAL CENTER, MORE THAN ONE MILLION CHILDREN CAN RELY ON WMC'S COMPREHENSIVE PEDIATRIC SPECIALTIES. TO BETTER MEET THE REGION'S INCREASING NEEDS, THE BRAND NEW MARIA FARERI CHILDREN'S HOSPITAL IS UNDER CONSTRUCTION, SCHEDULED FOR COMPLETION IN 2003.

The WMC STAT Flight team has two fully equipped Medevac helicopters, staffed around the clock with specially trained critical care nurses and paramedics. The team responds in minutes to accidents and other emergencies, swiftly delivering critically injured or ill infants, children, and adults to an appropriate medical facility while providing advanced medical care during transit. The STAT Flight team covers a 5,000-square-mile region, carrying out more than 1,800 missions per year.

The WMC Burn Center—the only such center between New York City and the Canadian border—has been recognized as one of the premier burn centers in the nation by the American College of Surgeons and the American Burn Association. It incorporates the Advanced Wound Therapy and Hyperbaric Center, treating victims of fire and a wide variety of injuries and wounds.

The Zalmen A. Arlin Cancer Institute is dedicated to delivering comprehensive, advanced-level diagnostic, therapeutic, and support services to cancer patients. The institute has the region's only teaching hospital cancer program approved by the American College of Surgeons and offers the latest in cancer therapies, including bone marrow and stem cell transplants.

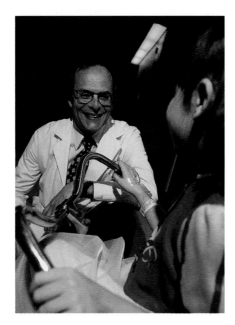

The Neuroscience Center at WMC offers specialized programs for some of the most complex medical cases, including adult and pediatric brain tumor treatment, pediatric neurosurgery, treatments for motion disorders, and a comprehensive epilepsy program. In addition, its specialized stroke service—one of only a few in the state—provides stroke victims with advanced care, from diagnosis and emergency treatment through inpatient care and rehabilitation.

LEADING-EDGE HEALTH CARE

At the forefront of medical technology, Westchester Medical Center recently became the fifth hospital in the nation to offer Novalis® Shaped Beam Surgery™, one of the least invasive, high-precision treatment options available for patients diagnosed with cancer, brain tumor, or neurologic or vascular disorders. This revolutionary system combines state-of-the-art radiosurgery and radiotherapy applications in a single integrated treatment plan.

Other technological advances at WMC include robotic surgery that enables minimally invasive surgical procedures. The robotic da Vinci™ Surgical System, presently in use for general and cardiac surgery, allows surgeons more precision, greater flexibility, and 3-D visualization that is similar to traditional surgery but provides better access and affords faster healing and less scarring for the patient.

Profiles
Manufacturing, R&D,

Photo: © CORBIS

THE AMERICAN SUGAR REFINING COMPANY/DOMINO FOODS, INC.

From its state-of-the-art headquarters in a historic Yonkers sugar refinery, one of the world's largest vertically integrated sugar companies directs the operations that make the nation—and world—sweeter.

While America's business reportage at the start of the 21st century was riveted on a turbulent global economy and the grim spectacle of giant corporations imploding through mismanagement, many genuinely positive corporate accomplishments proceeded with great significance, if little fanfare. Among them was the consolidation in November 2001 of Refined Sugars Inc. and Domino Sugar.

The new enterprise, which combines the resources of four component organizations into one of the largest sugar operations in the nation, bears the well-known name of Domino Sugar. Domino now integrates sugar farming, processing, and marketing functions under one management team headquartered in Yonkers, New York. The two principal divisions operating from Yonkers are The American Sugar Refining Company, responsible for sugar production, and Domino Foods, Inc., which markets the output of The American Sugar Refining Company and Okeelanta Corporation. With a daily refining capacity of approximately 16.5 million pounds, Domino Foods ranks as the largest single marketer of refined cane sugar in the United States.

ABOVE ARE EXAMPLES OF VARIOUS DOMINO SUGAR PACKAGES OFFERED AS PART OF THE EXTENSIVE DOMINO LINE OF PRODUCTS PRODUCED FOR CONSUMERS.

The present consolidation culminated a series of acquisitions that included British and Canadian sugar operations by Flo-Sun, the parent of the Fanjul family corporate group, which includes Florida Crystals. Under the guidance of Alfonso and J. Pepe Fanjul, the privately held, diversified agricultural, real estate, resort, and power generating group maintains operations and holdings in the United States, the Dominican Republic, and Europe. A vital partner in the new Domino Sugar organization is the Sugar Cane Growers Cooperative of Florida, which represents 56 Florida sugar cane growers. Companies controlled by the Fanjuls now own 63 percent of Domino Sugar; the Sugar Cane Growers Cooperative of Florida, 37 percent.

A REFINED HISTORY

Including its refining operations in New York, Maryland, and Louisiana, the company produces more than two million tons of refined sugar and specialty products a year

One of five production facilities operated by The American Sugar Refining Company (formally, Refined Sugars, Inc.), the Yonkers, New York, refinery is corporate headquarters for The American Sugar Refining Company and Domino Foods, Inc.

and generates annual revenues in excess of $1 billion. Corporate headquarters are located at the historic sugar refinery and administrative facilities that have been a part of the Yonkers industrial scene for most of the 20th century. Indeed, the city's first refinery—the Underhill and Wearing facility, which extracted brown sugar from molasses—was built in 1862. Historians note that sugar refining is probably the oldest continuing industry in Westchester County, and the Yonkers location, near the Port of New York, combines a superior waterfront, excellent railroad access, and an outstanding labor pool.

The idea for a liquid sugar plant originated in 1925 in a small molasses-and-refineries' syrup blending plant in Brooklyn called Tru-Cane Products. Daniel Wadsworth, a partner in Tru-Cane, recognized and developed the potential of liquid sugar by several means, but especially through the utilization of activated carbon to produce a high purity product that could be sold directly to food processors.

Capitalization of a new company, Refined Syrups, in Brooklyn, followed in 1927. In 1937 Refined Syrups purchased a Yonkers property that had housed a Spreckles sugar refinery and updated it, creating a modern liquid sugar plant. In 1938 granulated sugar capabilities were added, and the company changed its name to Refined Syrups & Sugars. The steady expansion and sophistication of the refinery over the years have brought numerous changes, including comprehensive computer controls for all phases of processing and packaging. Today the facility is among the industry's most modern.

SWEETENING THE POT—OR CUP

Domino's sugar is delivered to four market sectors: the food and beverage industry, food service, consumers, and the export trade. The food and beverage industry, which includes bakeries, confectioneries, dairies, food processors, and canneries, utilizes quantities from 100-pound bags to railcar lots in granulated, powdered, and brown variants as well as liquid sugar. Food service companies deliver food items to restaurants, hotels, schools, and other institutional consumers. The immense consumer market, which includes supermarket chains and other retail outlets of every kind, is where the familiar white, brown, and powdered sugars are found, in diverse sizes and packaging, for home baking and cooking—and coffee cups across the land. Finally, the export trade moves sugar most commonly in 50-kilo bags destined predominantly for Caribbean countries and Mexico.

As one of the world's largest vertically integrated sugar companies, Domino is poised to play an increasingly dynamic role in the betterment of not only the markets it serves but the many communities that support its activities.

Profiles

Media &

Photo: © CORBIS

LIGHTPATH

Lightpath, a service of Cablevision Systems Corporation, provides integrated voice, data, Internet, and video communications services for businesses in New York, New Jersey, and Connecticut.

Lightpath, a service of Cablevision Systems Corporation, owns, installs, and operates one of the nation's most advanced fiber-optic communications networks—more than 12,000 route miles of fiber-optic cable with some 66,000 access lines connecting more than 1,200 commercial buildings. From its Jericho, New York, headquarters, the company offers comprehensive communications services for virtually fail-safe voice, data, Internet, and video capabilities for businesses in New York, New Jersey, and Connecticut.

While most other telecommunications companies remain dependent upon older technologies, from its launch in 1988 Lightpath has built and managed an advanced fiber-optic network to support the expanding needs of its customers' businesses: high standards of performance were literally built into Lightpath's robust infrastructure. That early planning ensured leadership by Lightpath in communications services well into the 21st century.

Lightpath distinguishes itself from other local exchange carriers (LECs) by building and delivering innovative communication solutions to meet the special needs of such industries as health care, finance, education, and government. As a facilities-based service provider, as opposed to a service reseller, Lightpath is able to drive significant value to its customers, who can save as much as 30 percent in comparison to similar offerings from other providers.

Lightpath's all-digital, 100 percent fiber-optic network is built with today's most advanced communications technologies and features partnerships with industry-leading companies, including Lucent Technologies for voice communications and

Lightpath Intelligent Optical Network

Lightpath
A Service of Cablevision
The communications of tomorrow. Today.

LEGEND
● LIGHTPATH HUB
— FIBER BACKBONE
Ⓐ 5ESS & ATM SWITCH

SERVING WESTCHESTER COUNTY AND THE TRI-STATE AREA, LIGHTPATH'S ALL-DIGITAL, 100 PERCENT FIBER-OPTIC NETWORK EXTENDS THROUGHOUT WESTCHESTER, LONG ISLAND, NEW YORK CITY, NORTHERN NEW JERSEY, AND SOUTHERN CONNECTICUT.

switching, Cisco Systems for powered fiber-rich data and Internet networking, and Checkpoint software for enhanced security and monitoring. To maintain its advantage, Lightpath continually evaluates and integrates new approaches to proven transmission technologies.

Cablevision's operations range from cable television packages that serve more than three million metropolitan New York households to national television networks such as American Movie Classics; Bravo; MSG, which includes the New York Knicks and the New York Rangers; and Fox Sports Net.

Its parent company's 30-year presence in the New York metropolitan area and proven performance back Lightpath's solid commitment to the New York region well into this new millennium.

Photo: © CORBIS

Profiles

Photo: © CORBIS

COLLINS BROTHERS MOVING CORPORATION

Award-winning Collins Brothers Moving Corporation provides household and commercial moving and storage services on a local, long-distance, and international basis.

BECAUSE OF COLLINS BROTHERS MOVING CORPORATION'S DEEP COMMITMENT TO SERVICE, CUSTOMERS CAN EXPECT A HIGH LEVEL OF PROFESSIONALISM IN EVERY MOVE THE COMPANY HANDLES.

Collins Brothers Moving Corporation's roots are solidly established in Westchester County. The company was founded in picturesque Larchmont, New York, in 1910 by William Collins, who moved furniture in Westchester and New York City via horse and wagon. In 1958, his sons, Hugh and William Collins, took over the business, incorporated it, and began handling household relocations.

In 1972, the company was purchased from the Collins brothers by Frank E. Webers, Collins Brothers owner and chief executive officer. Webers has taken the firm from a two-truck, three-employee operation to a company with over 150 vehicles and 350 employees.

AWARD-WINNING SERVICES

Today, Collins Brothers, which is also an agent for Atlas Van Lines, is one of the New York metropolitan area's largest moving and storage companies. It is a full-service organization, handling household and commercial work both domestically and internationally.

In recent years, Collins Brothers has developed a hospitality division which handles the receipt, storage, delivery, and installation of products for the hotel industry during renovation or new construction projects.

Being an Atlas agent enables Collins Brothers to provide customers with moving and storage throughout the United States and abroad, by networking with other Atlas agents. Collins Brothers is one of the largest Atlas agents and consistently wins awards for packing, hauling, and customer satisfaction. In 2001, Collins Brothers was once again awarded the most coveted Atlas award, the Milton M. Hill Quality Award. The award requires the mover to exceed world-class goals in more than 12 categories, ranging from customer satisfaction ratings and weight estimating accuracy to claims ratios, safety points, and warehouse ratings.

SECURE, MODERN, STATE-OF-THE-ART FACILITIES

Collins Brothers maintains its original corporate headquarters in Larchmont at 620 Fifth Avenue, with a 12,500-square-foot facility. The company also operates a 136,000-square-foot storage facility in Brewster, New York, which provides customers with state-of-the-art, clean, modern, temperature-controlled warehousing, including a security alarm and sprinkler systems.

In addition to its Larchmont and Brewster facilities, Collins Brothers has a 23,000-square-foot warehouse in Long Island City, which serves commercial clients in New York City. Household goods and office furnishings are stored in specially designed storage vaults, and rack storage is available for record retention and storage of oversize items.

In May 1999, Collins Brothers opened a moving division in Irving, Texas, just 10 miles outside of Dallas. This division, with a 38,000-square-foot warehouse, handles household and commercial office moving and storage to and from the Dallas area.

In February 2001, Collins Brothers opened another moving division, in Southampton, New York. This division handles high-end relocation moves to and from New York City and also places a strong emphasis on storage. The storage emphasis has necessitated the opening of additional storage facilities in Southampton, Riverhead, and Bridgehampton.

PROFESSIONAL, QUALITY SERVICE

Quality has always been the Collins Brothers goal, dating back to 1910 when the company was founded, and Webers strives to maintain a reputation based on providing Collins Brothers customers with professional, quality service.

"Maintaining this reputation would not be possible without the fine staff at Collins Brothers," Webers says, "for staff members are the company's representatives, the service providers, and the ones who keep our customers coming back over and over again."

ABOVE: WHETHER CUSTOMERS HAVE 2,000 OR 2,000,000 SQUARE FEET OF GOODS TO BE MOVED, THEY ENJOY PEACE OF MIND WITH THE PROFESSIONAL SERVICES OF COLLINS BROTHERS. BELOW: AT COLLINS BROTHERS, "CUSTOMER SATISFACTION IS OUR GOAL AND HAS BEEN OUR GOAL SINCE 1910."

THE COUNTY CHAMBER OF COMMERCE, INC.

The County Chamber of Commerce, Inc., serves to further local economic vitality and help the businesses of Westchester County succeed, offering its members a variety of programs and valuable information sources.

The County Chamber of Commerce, Westchester's largest business organization for close to 100 years, serves the diverse and dynamic business community of Westchester County. The chamber's seven hundred–plus members represent a wide range of business and community organizations—including major companies among the top 100 of the Fortune 500, financial institutions, and high-tech, manufacturing, retail, and nonprofit enterprises, as well as entrepreneurial small businesses. Whatever the size of the business, the County Chamber serves to help business succeed.

The County Chamber's achievements are a result of a multitude of efforts by its members. The work they accomplish is reflected in the chamber's councils, committees, and task forces:

- The Small Business Council focuses on the special needs of owners of small businesses. Programs— from information forums and networking events to the Academy for Entrepreneurial Excellence to Executive Dialogue—are created by council members working together to develop new opportunities for small businesses to grow.
- The Economic Development Council's Ambassador's Club reaches out to County Chamber members to understand the products and services they provide and to identify their business needs. The council also proactively focuses on the results of economic development in Westchester County.
- The Human Resources (HR) Council is a network of HR professionals who provide information to each other as well as to other chamber members. The HR Council also works on wage and salary surveys and workforce recruitment and retention.
- The Area Development Council addresses public policies that affect Westchester's economic competitiveness, including housing and transportation for the county's workforce, workforce development, and taxation.
- The Governmental Action Council's advocacy role includes interaction with legislators through

AT THE FIRST ANNUAL FINANCIAL FORECAST OF THE COUNTY CHAMBER OF COMMERCE ARE, FROM LEFT, DENNIS B. KREMER, CHAIRMAN 2002; MARSHA GORDON, PRESIDENT/CEO; RON INSANA, CO-ANCHOR, CNBC "BUSINESS CENTER"; AND T. DANIEL TEARNO, CHAIRMAN 2001.

Candidates Forums and trips to Albany and Washington, D.C. The County Chamber also has a Political Action Committee that proactively supports pro-business candidates.

- The Technology Council serves as a conduit to technology resources and provides timely and relevant information to County Chamber members. Technology is integrated into the mission of all chamber councils, to keep Westchester's leading business organizations on the cutting edge.

The chamber's membership is growing day by day because Westchester County businesses recognize that the County Chamber exists to help them do business.

Each and every member not only benefits from the information the chamber provides, but also becomes part of the network of networks at the County Chamber.

The County Chamber of Commerce staff and board of directors welcome businesses to participate in the chamber and gain the strategic business advantages enjoyed by its members. Most of all, by joining the County Chamber, each business adds a voice in the effort to enhance the economic vitality of Westchester County.

Photo: © CORBIS

Profiles

Tourism,

Photo: © CORBIS

THE CROWNE PLAZA HOTEL

The Crowne Plaza Hotel in White Plains provides finely appointed guest rooms and suites with exceptional amenities and services, as well as state-of-the-art event spaces for meetings and elegant social occasions.

The Crowne Plaza Hotel in White Plains has earned a reputation for providing superior service to business and pleasure travelers alike. Built in 1985 in downtown White Plains, the Crowne Plaza's 14 floors include 401 elegantly appointed guest rooms and two suites, and 17,000 square feet of flexible meeting and event space.

Providing exceptional service has long been a cornerstone of the hotel's mission, and the Crowne Plaza White Plains is winner of the prestigious Quality Excellence award. Key to the hotel's outstanding service is its long-standing staff, many of whom have been with the hotel since it opened.

Historically, the hotel has maintained an average occupancy of 85 percent. Individual and group business travelers fill the hotel during the week. On weekends, the hotel is the place to be for leisure travelers attending social functions. In addition to its corporate and leisure clientele, the hotel has hosted notable groups such as the Professional Golf Association (PGA) and the Ladies Professional Golf Association (LPGA).

Crowne Plaza's guest rooms are especially luxurious thanks to a 2002 renovation that added numerous features, such as marble bath facilities. All rooms include such amenities as a coffeemaker, refreshment center, hair dryer, iron and ironing board, business desk with ergonomically designed desk chair, two telephone lines including a data port, and an in-room safe.

Guests looking for added luxury can take advantage of the Club Level. The Club Level offers the privacy of keyed access, nightly turndown service, bathrobes, and access to the Club Lounge. The lounge provides a complimentary continental breakfast and evening cocktails and hors d'oeuvres. The club's suites feature spacious living and dining rooms with bedrooms on either side.

All guests can enjoy hotel facilities such as the indoor swimming pool and whirlpool spa, as well as

IN THE CROWNE PLAZA LOBBY AT THE MAIN ENTRANCE, BRASS, COPPER, AND STEEL COME TOGETHER IN THIS DRAMATIC SCULPTURE, WHICH IS SUSPENDED FROM THE SKYLIGHTS.

a private-access fitness center that is open 24 hours per day. Fenimore's Bistro serves a variety of delicious dishes for breakfast, lunch, and dinner. The Sunday brunch and Saturday night prime rib buffet are favorites among local patrons. A private dining room accommodates up to 30 people, and room service is available daily until midnight. Guests also will find more than 60 great dining opportunities within walking distance of the hotel.

The Crowne Plaza Hotel's transportation service is extensive, providing guests with rides to and from local businesses, shops, and restaurants within a seven-mile radius. The hotel's vans also shuttle guests to and from the Westchester County Airport.

Crowne Plaza is a lavish venue for events, from corporate conferences to weddings, bar and bat mitzvahs, and reunions of all types. A full-time support team of catering and conference managers is available to assist with the planning of business meetings and special occasions, and a banquet manager is on duty to provide personal service throughout all functions.

The hotel's meeting and banquet event space of 17,000 square feet accommodates groups of up to 800 people. Seventeen meeting rooms include a boardroom

ABOVE: THE HOTEL'S GUEST ROOMS, COMPLETELY RENOVATED IN 2002, INCORPORATE WARM TONES IN AN ELEGANT AND MODERN DESIGN. BELOW LEFT: THE MAMARONECK BOARDROOM PROVIDES AN INTIMATE SETTING FOR EXECUTIVE MEETINGS.

with a beautiful handcrafted oak conference table and 16 ergonomic leather chairs. The New Rochelle Ballroom accommodates up to 800 people for meetings and up to 600 for dining. Hosts may choose from a variety of menus or the hotel's trained catering experts can create a special menu.

Crowne Plaza conference facilities feature technologically advanced audio-visual equipment. Meeting rooms are equipped with in-room climate controls, category 5 shielded cable with multiple port capabilities, and high-speed Internet access. The hotel's in-house audio-visual department offers a comprehensive range of equipment and services, including microphones, slide projectors, VCR, LCD computer-display lecture facilities, modem connections and high-speed ISDN lines, Web-casting, and satellite communication networks for worldwide videoconferencing capabilities. Secretarial, fax, and copying services are available in the hotel's business center.

Its state-of-the-art facilities are a testament to the Crowne Plaza White Plains commitment to provide exceptional service and value to all of its guests, whether visiting for business or for pleasure.

ANTUN'S OF WESTCHESTER

A premier catering facility, Antun's of Westchester offers its patrons spectacular indoor and outdoor settings and provides delicious four-star cuisine for events, from small gatherings to grand celebrations.

A Victorian mansion centered in the heart of beautiful Westchester County provides the perfect backdrop for one of the premier catering facilities in New York. Owned and operated by award-winning chef Ronald J. Stytzer, Antun's of Westchester, in Elmsford, has evolved over the past two decades to epitomize the ultimate in culinary experiences.

Every event is made special by the European-trained Antun's staff, which weaves its magic into each affair with the help of a variety of picturesque settings. A rolling lawn next to a babbling brook, a romantic lily pond with a Japanese bridge, or, reminiscent of an earlier era, a white gazebo nestled amid elegant gardens —all are available outdoor venues. Inside, a stately ballroom with a welcoming fireplace and beautiful garden views creates a luxurious atmosphere.

ABOVE: AN OUTDOOR WEDDING CEREMONY TAKES PLACE IN ONE OF THE PICTURESQUE GARDENS OF PREMIER CATERER, ANTUN'S OF WESTCHESTER, IN ELMSFORD. BELOW: AWARD-WINNING CHEF RONALD STYTZER OWNS AND OPERATES ANTUN'S, WHICH ALSO OFFERS ELEGANT INTERIOR SETTINGS, INCLUDING A STATELY BALLROOM.

Antun's four-star cuisine includes a variety of delicious dishes, specially prepared, and nontraditional custom-created menus are available. Whether enjoying a famous Antun's brunch or garden party, or planning an event—from an intimate get-together to a grand-scale wedding or other celebration—patrons of Antun's receive individual attention, with zealous commitment to detail.

Representing the United States, chef/owner Stytzer won the gold medal at the 1980 International Culinary Olympics in Frankfurt, Germany. He has received many other highly recognized awards, including the prestigious Raymond Vaudard Medal of Excellence from the Chefs de Cuisine Association of America, in 2000. Stytzer also owns and operates M. C. Food Service, located on two Mercy College campuses—Dobbs Ferry and the Bronx.

An active member of the Long Island Culinary Association, the New York Guild of Chefs, the Vatel Club, and the Chefs de Cuisine Association of America, Stytzer also is a member of the Westchester County Chamber of Commerce, serving on the board of directors since 1999. President of the Westchester and Rockland Chapter of the New York State Restaurant Association, Stytzer also has served as chairman of the board of the New York State Restaurant Association. He is a member of the National Restaurant Association and was presented with its Award of Special Recognition for Dedicated Service in the Food Service Industry, in 1997. In 2001, Stytzer was nominated to be chairman of the Elmsford Business Association.

"I have the privilege to be a part of a very gratifying business where it is an honor to routinely share in the happy occasions of neighbors and friends throughout Westchester County," Stytzer says.

LILLIAN VERNON CORPORATION

Leading mail order and on-line retailer Lillian Vernon offers thousands of delightful, unique gifts and personalized products for the home, garden, and office.

Lillian Vernon Corporation is a leading catalog and on-line retailer that markets 6,000 gift, housewares, gardening, children's, and Christmas products.

The company was founded by Lillian Vernon, chairman and chief executive officer. Vernon and her family fled Germany prior to World War II and settled in New York City. She started her company on her kitchen table in 1951 with $2,000 of wedding gift money. The business was launched in Mount Vernon, New York, with a $495 advertisement for a personalized handbag and belt in *Seventeen* magazine that generated $32,000 in orders.

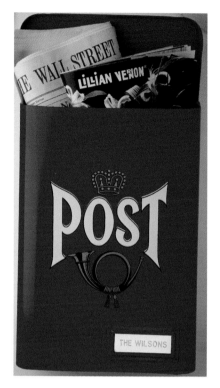

Today, more than 45 million Americans are familiar with the Lillian Vernon name. The company is well known for offering unique merchandise and exceptionally good values. The average product retails for $28.50, and the average customer order is $56.50.

Headquartered in Rye, Lillian Vernon publishes eight catalog titles: *Lillian Vernon*, *Sales & Bargains*, *Lilly's Kids*, *Lillian Vernon Gardening*, *Personalized Gifts*, *Christmas Memories*, *Favorites*, and *Rue de France*. The catalogs average 96 pages containing more than 700 products.

Lillian Vernon mails more than 169 million catalogs in 35 editions. In 2001, the company shipped more than 5.6 million packages and revenues totaled $287.1 million. At the height of the Christmas season, Lillian Vernon employs more than 5,300 people, including 150 representatives at the company's Seasonal Call Center in New Rochelle.

Lillian Vernon is a pioneer in offering free personalization, a company trademark. The company has one of the largest personalization departments in the country.

Lillian Vernon's on-line catalogs can be found at www.lillianvernon.com and www.ruedefrance.com. The company also sells corporate gifts, premiums, and incentives to the business-to-business markets. Lillian Vernon has 15 outlet stores, located in New York in Hartsdale, Brooklyn, Lake George, and Riverhead. Outlet stores are also in Delaware, South Carolina, Tennessee, and Virginia. There are two Rue de France stores in Rhode Island.

ABOVE: LILLIAN VERNON MAILS MORE THAN 169 MILLION CATALOGS A YEAR IN 35 EDITIONS. LEFT: LILLIAN VERNON, FOUNDER AND CHIEF EXECUTIVE OFFICER, IS A PIONEER IN THE DIRECT MARKETING INDUSTRY.

Profiles
Transportation

& Distribution

Photo: © CORBIS

MTA METRO-NORTH RAILROAD

Named one of the nation's premier railroads, MTA Metro-North Railroad continually pursues innovative service improvements to meet customers' rising expectations, while strategically planning and building for tomorrow.

Once the custodian of a crumbling infrastructure, the new millennium finds MTA Metro-North Railroad in an enviable position.

Today, heavy investments that were made to improve the railroad's physical plant have paid handsome dividends. Not only has ridership increased to a record level, but Metro-North has been selected the premier railroad in the nation three times in the past decade.

Metro-North is responsible for five commuter lines serving nine counties in two states. The railroad directly operates the Hudson, Harlem, and New Haven lines from its flagship station, the world-renowned Grand Central Terminal. It also is responsible for the Port Jervis and Pascack Valley lines out of Hoboken Terminal in New Jersey under a service agreement.

More than 240,000 trips are taken on 617 trains from 120 stations daily. For the past decade, the railroad's on-time performance has been extremely strong, standing above 96 percent for the past four years.

Financial performance is equally strong. Approximately 60 percent of the railroad's expenses are covered by passenger revenue and rents. This number has been among the best in the industry for nearly a decade.

In quarterly surveys, Metro-North's customers routinely give service an approval rating of 7.5 to 7.9 out of a possible score of 10. Service improvements plus customer satisfaction have yielded ridership increases. The railroad now carries more than 71.9 million riders annually, the highest ridership in 50 years. Ridership growth in 2000 was 5 percent—over four million new rides. The railroad has captured the lion's share of the peak commuter market to Manhattan—approximately 80 percent—and that share continues to grow.

Rather than rest on its laurels, Metro-North realizes that it has to continue to build on its success—and not become a victim of it.

LOOKING AHEAD

Moving forward requires constant planning. Metro-North identifies its needs not just for today, but for up to 20 years in the future as well.

ABOVE LEFT: SHOWN HERE IS GRAND CENTRAL TERMINAL'S MAIN CONCOURSE, WITH ITS FAMOUS "ZODIAC" CEILING. BELOW: A GENESIS LOCOMOTIVE TRAVELS ALONG THE UPPER HUDSON RIVER, WITH A VIEW OF BANNERMAN'S ISLAND. PHOTOS © FRANK ENGLISH/MTA METRO-NORTH RAILROAD

By mapping out a long-term strategy, Metro-North develops major projects to improve service, identifies the funding requirements of those projects, and plans how best to pay for and perform the work.

Continued investment in the railroad's infrastructure and equipment also is essential. Through 2004, the MTA and the New York State legislature have earmarked more than $1.3 billion in capital funding to maintain and improve Metro-North.

Some $521 million—39 percent of that entire allocation—will be used to purchase new railcars or to rehabilitate the existing fleet to extend its useful life.

The fleet needs to be maintained, so $139 million has been set aside to rebuild maintenance shops and yards.

More than $200 million is targeted for track renewal work—rail, ties, interlockings, and turnouts. There is also a significant amount of money earmarked to rebuild bridges and maintain signal and power systems.

As ridership increases, so does a need for better station and parking facilities. Almost $300 million is allocated to renovating these "front doors" of the railroad's service.

Even after all this work, it still becomes important to expand capacity. Metro-North received funding that has enabled it to extend the railroad—as was the case in 2000 when the Wassaic Branch, the first extension of its service territory, was placed into service in neighboring Dutchess County. The railroad will also be able to squeeze more track capacity within its existing footprint by building a third track in the densely traveled two-track segment of its mid-Harlem Line in Westchester.

ABOVE: MTA METRO-NORTH'S NEW WASSAIC STATION IN DUTCHESS COUNTY SERVES THE RAILROAD'S WASSAIC BRANCH, WHICH WAS COMPLETED IN 2000 AS THE FIRST SERVICE TERRITORY EXTENSION. BELOW LEFT: AN M3 ELECTRIC CAR PROVIDES SERVICE ON METRO-NORTH'S UPPER HARLEM LINE. PHOTOS © FRANK ENGLISH/MTA METRO-NORTH RAILROAD

NEW SERVICES FOR CUSTOMERS

While investment programs are essential to Metro-North's future, the railroad is still aggressive about reducing its reliance on government subsidies by increasing ridership, sometimes in nontraditional ways.

Building ridership during the Reverse Peak, Off Peak, and Weekend service segments has, in part, driven growth, which has reached record levels. Where parking limitations pose a problem to attracting new customers, alternatives such as bus, van, and even ferry services provide access to stations.

The railroad continues to explore new ways to meet customers' rising expectations. WebTicket, a new on-line ticket-purchasing service, allows customers to buy most ticket types with the click of a computer mouse. New ticket vending machines accept credit or debit cards as well as cash. A computerized Customer Information Center now enables railroad representatives to provide the most up-to-the-minute travel information quickly and accurately. In addition, a modern and comfortable Customer Service Center has been opened in Grand Central Terminal.

It is going to take continuing innovations such as these, along with a solid infrastructure and a dedicated team of employees, to meet ever-changing customer expectations and deal with the effects of a turbulent economy in this new century. MTA Metro-North is ready for the challenge.

HEINEKEN USA

In the tradition of an enlightened business, Heineken USA, headquartered in White Plains, pursues the highest standards in making quality beers and is committed to corporate responsibility in the community.

HEINEKEN USA'S PORTFOLIO OF WORLD-CLASS BRANDS OF BEER INCLUDES HEINEKEN LAGER BEER, HEINEKEN SPECIAL DARK BEER, BUCKLER NONALCOHOLIC BREW, AND AMSTEL LIGHT.

What is a nice Dutch beer company doing in a place like Westchester County? A lot of good things, to be sure.

Heineken USA, the largest beer importer in the United States, has its headquarters in White Plains and has done much to make its presence known in the county. Nearly everyone is familiar with the brand Heineken. In fact, it is one of the world's best known and most successful trademarks and the world's most international beer, sold in more than 170 countries. From Australia to Zimbabwe, Heineken is the world standard for beer.

So, what about the company's place in Westchester and what does it mean to the county?

HEINEKEN USA'S BEGINNINGS
The story of Heineken USA is fairly recent history. The brand has been sold in America continuously since the repeal of Prohibition in 1933. How it came to the United States at that time is an interesting yarn in itself. A Dutch-American ship's steward named Leo van Munching became acquainted with one Henri Pierre Heineken during a transatlantic crossing, shortly before the end of Prohibition. As the

beer industry was soon to find out, van Munching was quite a salesman, as he persuaded Heineken to award him the exclusive U.S. importing rights to Heineken beer. This was a time when the American beer business was mostly a local affair, when every city of any size had at least one—and often several—breweries. It was unlikely that the strong loyalty enjoyed by local brands would be diminished by a foreign liquid. Van Munching persevered, however, and quickly built a highly successful business.

In 1991, Heineken NV, the brand's owner, agreed to purchase the U.S. company from van Munching's son, Leo van Munching Jr. Heineken took over management control of van Munching and Company in 1994 and renamed the company "Heineken USA" in 1995. That year was meaningful to Westchester, as well, because in April, Heineken USA left Manhattan, moving to 50 Main Street in White Plains. In November of 2000, the company doubled its space, moving to the Reckson Metro Center on Hamilton Avenue.

CORPORATE CITIZENSHIP
Heineken fervently believes in being a good corporate citizen and feels strongly about responsibility. As an alcohol beverage company, Heineken USA believes that it has a responsibility to make, market, and sell its

products in a responsible fashion. It is meticulous about integrity in advertising and is careful about the properties used to market its brands. Unlike many other beer companies, it does not sponsor motor sports activities. It also avoids sponsorship of professional teams.

DRINKING RESPONSIBLY

The company is also committed to responsible alcohol consumption, a value that goes back to its founder, Gerard Adriaan Heineken. In 1863, Heineken started the company by purchasing a nearly 300-year-old brewery in Amsterdam. One of the key reasons for the purchase was his concern over the irresponsible consumption of distilled spirits. Heineken wanted to provide a viable and more moderate alternative alcoholic beverage. Today, Heineken USA has a Corporate Alcohol Policy, which was originally developed by the Dutch parent company and adapted for the U.S. operating company.

The company also has an Alcohol and Work Policy that governs employee behavior at work and work-related events. Among the precepts of this policy is the statement that employees are always representatives of the company and should be moderate in their consumption behavior at all times. In addition, the company requires all its employees to be certified in the TIPS training program; "TIPS" is short for Training in Intervention Procedures for Servers of Alcohol. No other alcohol beverage company has made this commitment to employee education about the products it sells.

The company has also established the Heineken USA SAFE CALL™ program, a national initiative to help bars and restaurants reduce drunk driving by giving consumers an easy way to use pay phones without cost to call a local taxi company, to be driven home safely. The program is available from coast to coast and has been praised by many businesses and groups as a reasonable and effective way to reduce the problem of drunk driving.

SAFE CALL™
Heineken
ENJOY HEINEKEN RESPONSIBLY.™
1·800 TAXICAB
800 829 4222

THE Heineken
MUSIC INITIATIVE *MAKING A DIFFERENCE THROUGH MUSIC*

ABOVE: THE HEINEKEN MUSIC INITIATIVE IS AN INNOVATIVE EFFORT TO PLACE A GREATER FOCUS ON URBAN MUSIC AND TO BENEFIT UP-AND-COMING MUSICIANS IN THE URBAN COMMUNITY. IT IS A NONPROFIT ORGANIZATION THAT DEVELOPS A MUSIC CD EACH YEAR WITH BOTH ESTABLISHED AND UNSIGNED ARTISTS, FOCUSING ON A SINGLE MUSIC GENRE—FOR EXAMPLE, NEO-SOUL. A PORTION OF THE PROCEEDS IS DONATED TO THE VH1 SAVE THE MUSIC FOUNDATION, WHICH PROVIDES FUNDING TO MUSIC EDUCATION PROGRAMS IN INNER CITY SCHOOLS. BELOW: THE HEINEKEN USA SAFE CALL™ PROGRAM IS DESIGNED TO HELP BARS AND RESTAURANTS REDUCE DRUNK DRIVING BY ENABLING CONSUMERS TO MAKE FREE CALLS TO LOCAL TAXI COMPANIES AND BE SAFELY DRIVEN HOME.

DIVERSITY—A KEY TO SUCCESS

Heineken USA believes that diversity of talent and of thought are important to continuing success. The company developed a broad-based diversity initiative, which included the establishment of a Diversity Council, made up of employees from around the nation, from all levels and all walks of life. This council has been instrumental in providing a solid agenda of training and developing a new mindset about the importance of diversity to the company.

Putting these ideas into practice, the company has formed partnerships with five National Urban League affiliates around the nation where Heineken USA has facilities. Named the "Rising Star" initiative, the program works with these affiliates, in Atlanta, Chicago, Los Angeles, New York, and Westchester County, to bring diverse candidates to the company. The program helps include diversity in the process of increasing the company's workforce, due to continuing sales growth. Reaching out to the community in this way and with many other organizations helps Heineken USA ensure that it understands the culture and values of all its consumers and that it contributes to the betterment of particular constituencies who strongly support Heineken USA.

What is ahead for Heineken USA? More success, more growth, and more good things in "a place like Westchester County."

Bibliography

PRINT SOURCES

Bird, Christiane. *New York State Handbook*. Emeryville, CA: Moon Travel Handbooks, 2000

County Trust Company Bank Note. "That's William L. Butcher." 11 (July 1957): 4–5, 7–8.

Westchester County. *An Economic Development Guide to Westchester County*. Elmsford, NY: Suburban Publishing, 2001

—— Business Journal. *The 2001 Book of Business Lists*. White Plains: Westchester County Business Journal, 2001.

—— Office of Economic Development. *Techonomy*. Published monthly.

—— Office of Tourism. *Annual Report 2000*.

WEB SITES

Abigail Kirsch Culinary Productions. <http://www.abigailkirsch.com> (July 25, 2001)

Acorda Therapeutics. <http://www.acorda.com> (July 20, 2001)

Atlas Air. <http://www.atlasair.com> (June 21, 2001)

Bleakley Platt & Schmitt. <http://www.bpslaw.com> (June 21, 2001)

Bloedbeld, Louis. "The Rise of Bakelite and Other Plastics in the USA during the 1930s." <http://www.let.ruu.nl/ams/xroads/bakelite.htm> (May 20, 2001)

Blythedale Children's Hospital. <http://www.blythedale.org> (June 21, 2001)

City of New Rochelle. "An Overview of the City of New Rochelle." <http://www.newrochelleny.com/textover.html> (May 16, 2001)

——Rye. "General Information and History." <http://www.ci.rye.ny.us/history.htm> (May 16, 2001)

——Yonkers. "A brief history of Yonkers." <http://www.cityofyonkers.com/history.html> (May 16, 2001)

College of New Rochelle. <http://www.cnr.edu> (June 23, 2001)

Consolidated Edison, Inc. <http://www.coned.com> (July 16, 2001)

Cuddy & Feder & Worby. <http://www.cfwlaw.com> (June 21, 2001)

Delfino Marketing Communications, Inc. <http://www.delfino.com> (June 21, 2001)

Eric Mowrer and Associates. <http://www.mower.com> (June 21, 2001)

Geritrex Corporation. <http://www.geritrex.com> (July 20, 2001)

"Governor Receives 'MVP' Award From Westchester Partnership." <http://www.state.ny.us/govrnor/press/april10_2_97.html > (July 20, 2001)

Greenwich Technology Partners. <http://www.greenwichtech.com> (June 21, 2001)

Healthcare Research Group. <http://www.corporateresearchgroup.com> (August 13, 2001)

"History of Kraft Foods." <http://inventors.about.com/library/inventors/blkraft.htm> (July 23, 2001)

"History of Westchester: Pre-History to 1783." <http://www.co.westchester.ny.us/history/1783.htm> (May 16, 2001)

"——1783–1865." <http://www.co.westchester.ny.us/history/1783.htm> (May 16, 2001)

"——1865–1920." <http://www.westchester.ny.us/history/1920.htm> (May 16, 2001)

"——1920–83." <http://www.co.westchester.ny.us/history/1983.htm> (May 16, 2001)

Hlotyak, Elizabeth. "Learning from a Distance." <http://www.businessjrnls.com/he/> (July 20, 2001)

——. "Westchester Community College Opens Biotech Center in Ossining." <http://westchestercountybusinessjournal.com/archives/news/040201e.htm> (July 20, 2001)

Hudson Valley Hospital Center. <http://www.hvhc.org > (June 25, 2001)

ImageWork Technologies Corporation. <http://www.imagewk.com> (June 21, 2001

International Paper Corporation. <http://www.internationalpaper.com> (July 16, 2001)

Iona College. <http://www.iona.edu > (May 20, 2001)

Irving, Washington. "The Legend of Sleepy Hollow." <http://www. jstudios.com/ravenscroft/sleepyhollow/legend.htm> (May 16, 2001)

Journal News. <http://www.thejournalnews.com> (August 13, 2001)

"Keeping It Local." <http://www.westchestergov.com/WITC/infoworld.htm> (July 23, 2001)

Khasru, B. Z. "Progenics, Regeneron on R&D Roller Coaster." <http://westchestercountybusinessjournal.com/tech/archive/0501_a.htm> (July 20, 2001)

——. "With Women in Mind." <http://www.westchestercountybusinessjournal.com/archives/focus/091100.htm> (July 20, 2001)

Landmark at Eastview. <http://www.lcorlandmark.com> (June 21, 2001)

Levy Institute Forecasting Center. <http://www.levyforecast.com> (August 13, 2001)

Metromedia Fiber Network, Inc. <http://www.mmfn.com> (June 21, 2001)

MTA (Metropolitan Transit Authority). <http://www.mta.nyc.ny.us> (July 16, 2001)

National Home Health Care Corporation. <http://www.nnhc.net/newyork.htm > (July 16, 2001)

New Roc City. <http://www.newroccity.net> (June 21, 2001)

"New Rochelle: The 20th Century . . . ." <http://www.newrochelleny.com/20thcentury.html> (May 16, 2001)

New York State Electric and Gas Company. <http://www.nyseg.com> (July 16, 2001)

"Newburgh's Resources." <http://www.newburgh-ny.com/nb_resource.htm> (August 13, 2001)

"Newspapers, Radio Stations, and Important Phone Numbers." <http://www.westchesterny.org/wccc81.htm > (July 20, 2001)

"Next Stop, New Roc City." <http://www.specialtyretail.net/issues/oct98/new%roc%city.htm > (May 16, 2001)

"Paul Loewenwarter." <http://www.cablevision.com/company/content/cor/editorials/wc/wc_bio.html> (August 13, 2001)

PepsiCo, Inc. <http://www.pepsico.com> (July 16, 2001)

Philippidis, Alex. "Biomed Scramble Heats Up." <http://westchestercounty businessjournal.com/archives/ledstory/030501.htm> (July 20, 2001)

——. "Biotech Breakout." <http://westchestercountybusinessjournal.com/tech/archive/0501_b.htm > (July 20, 2001)

——. "County, Cities Aim to Rebuild Manufacturing." <http:/westchester countybusinessjournal.com/archives/ledstory/081400.htm> (July 20, 2001)

——. "County Seeks $20 Million for Biotech Center." <http://www.westchester countybusinessjournal.com/archives/feature/021901.htm> (July 20, 2001)

Progenics Pharmaceuticals. <http://www.progenics.com> (June 21, 2001)

Purchase College, SUNY. <http://www.purchase.edu> (August 13, 2001)

Purdue Pharmaceuticals. <http://www.purduepharma.com> (July 20, 2001)

Regeneron Pharmaceuticals, Inc. <http://www.regneron.com> (June 21, 2001)

RSM McGladrey. <http://www.rsmmcgladrey.com> (June 21, 2001)

Rye Playland. <http://www.ryeplayland.org> (May 16, 2001)

Saint Vincent's Medical Center. <http://www.svcmc.org> (June 21, 2001)

Sarah Lawrence College. <http://www.slc.edu> (May 20, 2001)

Sleepy Hollow Chamber of Commerce. "History of the Tarrytown/Sleepy Hollow Area." <http://www.sleepyhollowchamber.com/history.html> (May 16, 2001)

Sound Shore Medical Center. <http://www.ssmc.org> (July 16, 2001)

Spano, Andrew J. "State of the County Address, 2001." <http://www.westchester gov.com/soc.htm> (August 13, 2001)

Starwood Hotels. <http://www.starwoodhotels.com> (June 21, 2001)

Suburban Street <http://www.suburbanstreet.com> (August 13, 2001)

Thalle Construction Company. "Projects—Corporate Headquarters." <http://www.thalle.com/projects/corporatehq.htm> (July 16, 2001)

"Thornton Wilder Page." <http://www.sky.net/~emily/thornton.html> (May 20, 2001)

Town of Ossining, NY. "Town History and Demographics." <http://townof ossining.com/info/hist-demos.htm> (May 16, 2001)

U. S. Census Bureau. "County Business Patterns." <http://www.census.gov/epcd/cbp/view/cbpview.html> (July 16, 2001)

——. "Westchester County, New York Quick Facts." <http://quickfacts.census.gov/qfd/states/36/36119.html> (July 16, 2001)

Village of Scarsdale. <http://www.village.scarsdale.ny.us> (May 16, 2001)

"Westchester Chooses Cablevision Lightpath to Build Westchester Telecom." <http://westchestergov.com/currentnews/westtelecom.htm> (May 20, 2001)

Westchester Commerce Magazine. <http://www.westchesterny.org/newsmag.htm> (July 20, 2001)

Westchester Community College. <http://www.sunywcc.edu> (June 23, 2001)

Westchester County. "Westchester County Economic Profile." <http://www.westchesterny.org/wccc85.htm> (July 16, 2001

—— Airport. <http://www.westchestergov.com/airport> (June 25, 2001)

—— Association. <http://www.westchester.org> (May 16, 2001)

—— Department of Economic Development. <http://www.westchestergov.com/economic/main.htm> (May 20, 2001)

—— Department of Planning. <http://www.westchester gov.com/planning/mainhome.htm> (May 20, 2001)

"Westchester County Education." <http://www.westchesterny.org/wccc82.htm> (July 20, 2001)

——. <http://www.co.westchester.ny.us/ed/main.htm> (May 16, 2001)

"Westchester County's Major Employers." <http://www.westchesterny.org/wcccc86a.htm > (July 20, 2001)

Westchester Medical Center. <http://worldclassmedicine.com> (June 21, 2001)

Westchester Wag. <http://www.westchesterwag.com> (August 13, 2001)

Wine Enthusiast Magazine. <http://www.wineenthusiastmag.com> (July 20, 2001)

Women's News. <http://ww.womensnewsonline.com> (August 13, 2001)

Yonkers Historical Society. <http://www.yonkershistory.org/infa.html> (May 16, 2001)

The Yonkers Marathon. <http://www.cityofyonkers.com/parks/marathon/> (May 16, 2001)

Index

Index